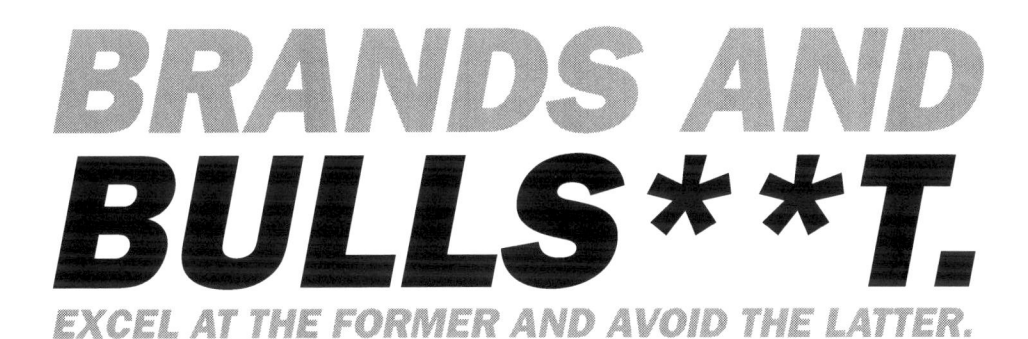

BRANDS AND BULLS**T.
EXCEL AT THE FORMER AND AVOID THE LATTER.
A BRANDING PRIMER FOR MILLENNIAL MARKETERS IN A DIGITAL AGE.

BERNHARD SCHROEDER

A Brand Expert Who Worked with Amazon, Yahoo, Apple and Nike

Author of Fail Fast & Simply Brilliant

BRANDS AND BULLST. EXCEL AT THE FORMER AND AVOID THE LATTER.**
A BRANDING PRIMER FOR MILLENNIAL MARKETERS IN A DIGITAL AGE.

PRAISE FOR BERNHARD SCHROEDER'S NEW BOOK ON BRANDING:

"For any digital marketer, strategist, creative or communicator in today's business world, read this book. Schroeder's career has spanned three decades and his branding knowledge is all here for the taking. Whether you're part of a startup or running an established Fortune 50 company, consider this the play book for how to compete in today's ever-changing world of brands."

TOM SUITER, CO-FOUNDER OF ENJOY, FORMER CREATIVE DIRECTOR, APPLE

"Brands and Bullsh*t examines the distinctions between branding and marketing - between tactics and strategy - for today's up-and-coming digital marketers. If you are looking to stand out in a crowded field, evolve into a well-rounded marketer or make the transition to brand marketing, you need to read this book."

SCOTT CARRINGTON, MGR, DIGITAL BRAND MARKETING, PATAGONIA

"Brands and Bulls**t should be mandatory reading for every online marketer. It's time you learned what you don't know about branding and step up to becoming a "bad ass" branding warrior."

THOM MCELROY, CO-FOUNDER, VOLCOM

"In my experience, too many new marketers confuse tactics for strategy and seem to believe communications somehow displaces the importance of branding. Brands and BullS**t is a comprehensive, career-enhancing course in the essentials of branding."

  MICHAEL IRWIN, FORMER CHIEF STRATEGY OFFICER, WD-40

"At Mirum, we create experiences that people want and businesses need. We work with companies who embrace the transformative power of digital. Brands and Bulls**t is a powerful addition to our digital branding arsenal."

  DANIEL KHABIE, GLOBAL CEO, MIRUM AGENCY

"In all that time that I have worked with some large brands, I've never worked with anyone who understands branding and where markets are going like Bernie Schroeder. He has the ability to look over the horizon and see where a brand needs to go to be successful. Brands and Bulls**t is not a book as much as it is a lighthouse in the darkness for young marketers."

  LEEANN IACINO, FORMER COO, BERKSHIRE HATHAWAY HOMESERVICES

BRANDS AND BULLST. EXCEL AT THE FORMER AND AVOID THE LATTER.**
A BRANDING PRIMER FOR MILLENNIAL MARKETERS IN A DIGITAL AGE.

As a digital marketer, are you marketing banner ads or building brands? Do you even know what a brand decision tree or a category ladder is? Probably not. Well, it's not your fault. You most likely grew up inside of a digital marketing environment. You had no brand mentor. However, your future career success depends on your ability to grow from being a digital marketer to becoming a brand expert.

*Brands and Bulls**t. Excel at the Former and Avoid the Latter* strips away the mystery of branding and gives you a branding primer necessary for every digital marketer. This new branding book offers you the insight and tools to learn how to excel at marketing strategy and branding. It is filled with over twenty years of expertise working with some of the best brands and branding experts in the world. Add wisdom, knowledge and value to your marketing career. This book will help you:

- Understand what branding in a digital world really means
- Learn how to create a powerful brand that creates a customer "feeling"
- Create specific brand strategies that really work in the marketplace
- Review ten possible brand strategies and understand their potential
- Understand how positioning and category ladders work and why
- Utilize tools like brand decision trees to simplify complex brand choices
- Create a branding strategy for a client or company that targets a blue ocean
- Begin to comprehend the NEW 4 P's of marketing and their impact
- Learn how to quickly create a brand plan with the BrandPlanr

Whether you work at a brand or work in an agency, you need to understand exactly how to build and lead a brand. You need to believe that to be a great marketer, you just need more branding insight and tools. And you definitely need to understand the difference between branding and bullshit. Achieve the marketing career you deserve. This is the branding primer every digital marketer has been waiting for. Enjoy.

For more information on this book or special orders, go to: www.bernieschroeder.com

View all Bernhard Schroeder titles at: Amazon.com, Barnes and Noble, Powell Books, Amacon Books, Audible.com, and wherever fine books are found.

Tired Coast Publishing
San Diego, California

This publication is designed to provide accurate and authoritative information in regard to the subject matter covered. It is sold with the understanding that the publisher is not engaged in rendering legal, accounting, or other professional service. If legal advice or other expert assistance is required, the services of a competent professional person should be sought.

© 2017 Bernhard Schroeder

All rights reserved.

Printed in the United States of America.

This publication may not be reproduced, stored in a retrieval system, or transmitted in whole or in part, in any form or by any means, electronic, mechanical, photocopying, recording, or otherwise, without the prior written permission of Tired Coast Publishing.

The scanning, uploading, or distribution of this book via the Internet or any other means without the express permission of the publisher is illegal and punishable by law. Please purchase only authorized electronic editions of this work and do not participate in or encourage piracy of copyrighted materials, electronically or otherwise. Your support of the author's rights is appreciated.

About Tired Coast Publishing

Tired Coast Publishing is a leader in talent development and advancing the skills of individuals to drive business success. Our mission is to support the goals of individuals and organizations through amazing books and research. Tired Coast Publishing's approach to improving personal performance combines experiential learning—learning through doing—with opportunities for ongoing professional growth at every step of one's career or journey.

" *IT'S NOT WHAT YOU **THINK** THAT MATTERS.*

*IT'S WHAT YOUR CUSTOMERS' **FEEL** THAT COUNTS.* "

> "Great companies that build an enduring brand have an emotional relationship with customers that has no barrier. And that emotional relationship is based on the most important characteristic, which is trust."
>
> **HOWARD SCHULTZ,** *STARBUCKS*

> "A brand for a company is like a reputation for a person. You earn reputation by trying to do hard things well. Your brand is what other people say about you when you're not in the room."
>
> **JEFF BEZOS,** *AMAZON*

CONTENTS
* * *

1 INTRODUCTION
BRANDING IN A DIGITAL WORLD.

8 CHAPTER ONE
CUSTOMERS CAN FEEL BUT MARKETERS NEED TO SEE.

23 CHAPTER TWO
BRANDING 101: AN OVERVIEW.

37 CHAPTER THREE
THE CHALLENGE OF BRANDING TODAY.

51 CHAPTER FOUR
THE BENEFITS OF BRANDING.

64 CHAPTER FIVE
THE STRATEGY BEHIND THE BRAND.

78 CHAPTER SIX
TEN BRAND BUILDING STRATEGIES.

89 CHAPTER SEVEN
BRAND ARCHITECTURE AND DECISION TREES.

102 *CHAPTER EIGHT*
THE ART OF POSITIONING A BRAND.

117 *CHAPTER NINE*
UNDERSTANDING MARKET CATEGORIES AND LADDERS.

128 *CHAPTER TEN*
TRENDS AND BLUE OCEANS MATTER.

144 *CHAPTER ELEVEN*
4 P'S OF MARKETING HAVE CHANGED.

152 *CHAPTER TWELVE*
BUILD A BRAND: THE POWER OF INTEGRATED MARKETING.

162 *CHAPTER THIRTEEN*
A BRAND PLANNER AND FINAL THOUGHTS.

169 *INDEX*

172 *ABOUT THE AUTHOR*

INTRODUCTION
BRANDING IN A DIGITAL WORLD.
✱ ✱ ✱

The founder of a digital marketing agency called me and pressed for a quick meeting as he had acquired a new client and was unsure about how to craft a marketing strategy for this particular company. He had stated on the phone that this client was more sophisticated and might need more than just online marketing solutions. We decided to have a lunch meeting to discuss his issue. As I walked on a street in downtown San Diego, I could see him approaching from the opposite direction and we both arrived at the restaurant at the same time. We were seated quickly and made small talk before he got serious.

 "I believe our agency is about to change significantly as we've just acquired our first really big client," he said. "The problem is that we are not sure about how to help this client strategically based on their situation." He then explained a bit more about the client including their products, the marketplace and the competition. After he answered a few of my questions, I was starting to get a sense of what the strategic problem or opportunity might be here.

He had founded his company four years earlier after gaining about three and a half years of marketing experience at several online marketing agencies in town. His digital marketing agency had grown very rapidly as had his client base. The agency had started with smaller clients but now they were attracting larger companies. Not exactly Fortune 500 companies but nevertheless, companies with revenues north of $50 to $100 million.

I had met him at San Diego State University, where I was teaching entrepreneurship and creativity courses, when he was a student and I had been a mentor to him over the past seven years. I knew him fairly well and quite frankly, I liked him. He had the attributes a marketing person and entrepreneur needed: He could sell, was not bothered by calculated risk and did not obsess about being perfect. He was constantly moving forward and learning "on the go." So, our meetings were usually spirited; we both had strong points of view on everything and were not afraid to voice our opinions. Maybe that's why we got along so well: Mutual passion and mutual respect.

I had spent twenty years in marketing becoming a branding expert to well-known, larger companies like Kellogg's, Mazda, American Express, Nikon, Apple, Yahoo and Amazon. So I quickly honed in on his agency's strategic issues with this client.

"It sounds like your client has a couple of options," I said to him. "They can re-position their brand in the marketplace to where customers are going and establish their leadership with this growing customer segment. Or they could create a new market category and position themselves on the first rung of the "product category ladder" in their customer's minds.", I stated. He stared at me for a few seconds and with a perplexed look on his face, he said, "What is re-positioning a brand, how do you establish a new market category and what the hell is a product category ladder?" Wow, I thought, these new digital marketers, with all their knowledge of on-line marketing do not know anything about branding. How are they olving complex branding issues? With bullshit? How did we get here?

WHY BRANDING IS THE ROCK STAR

Branding has infiltrated every corner of our universe it seems. Many consumers aren't consciously aware of it, but everything we buy, touch, eat, etc. has been thought through, analyzed, positioned, and presented in a certain way. Some of us may not be aware of how we regard certain companies and products but we have all been influenced to some extent by a company's branding efforts. Otherwise why would we pay $4 for a cup of coffee? Because it's not just coffee, it's a Starbucks coffee!

What's fascinating is that Millennials (read also digital marketers) are so affected by branding and yet they understand so very little about how branding actually happens or even how to create a brand. Branding is all around us. And if it's effective, it makes us feel something. Once we internalize that feeling, then we essentially "own" that brand. It becomes ours and we are not easily dissuaded to try or even buy another product. You don't need me to convince you that branding is valuable. Just look at all the companies that make products or provide services and dissect them down to what they actual provide: *Glass, metal, chips and software?* That's what makes up an Apple iPhone. But talk to a die-hard iPhone customer and this is what they will tell you, "I love my iPhone." *Love?* Needless to say, Apple has been extremely successful with their branding efforts. But, if branding is so important, how did we get to a place where digital marketers know so little about branding today?

THE MAGIC OF A MARKETING MERLIN

I spent twenty years crafting a marketing career that culminated in me being part of a five-person team that built a $1 billion integrated marketing agency with over 10,000 employees in more than thirty countries. After that I held Chief Marketing Officer roles in four successful company turnarounds. So, how did I—and just as importantly, how do you— become a marketing and branding expert?

You start at the bottom and work for some amazing marketing people, those whom I think of as "quasi Merlin's." Back in the 1980's, when I started my career, and for about fifty years before that, marketing was managed in a disciplined manner inside advertising and marketing agencies. There was structure in terms of who was at the bottom and who was at the top; there was training and there was a systematized progression of learning and experience. In other words, when you started, you started with small accounts and worked for bright people and you *learned*. If you were good, you moved up to bigger challenges. Early on, you were asked to say nothing in either company or client meetings and to learn how to listen and observe. If you were fortunate, someone would take you under their wings and start to explain the "unsaid" things that occurred in client meetings. Over time, you were asked to attend training programs on brand and marketing strategy so as to progress from being a "tactical" doer to a more "strategic" thinker. This usually took between five to seven years and about 10,000 hours. All of that mentoring, training and actual experience is what provided the basis for your strategic marketing education. It's what made you understand how critical brands were and that you could not really force anything onto the customer. That customers had to embrace your marketing messages and internalize all of that marketing to "feel" something. Hopefully that "something" is exactly what you wanted them to feel. I can't say "you need to love" your iPhone in my marketing. But I can say and project all the right things to make the customer say it and better yet "feel" it. That is the art and science of branding. So, why do most online marketers today not get the right kind of marketing strategy and branding training? Today's marketers are not dumb. On the contrary, they are pretty smart. So what has changed?

HOW THE INTERNET HAS CHANGED BRANDING

When I saw my first webpage in 1993, it was pretty unremarkable and made no real sense to me. Honestly, I did not think anything of it. Boy, was I wrong! Initially, the early Internet (backbone infrastructure) and the World Wide Web (graphics interface browser) was dominated by "pretty" websites (all graphics and photos, no real content or purpose) that really served as marketing brochures. All that changed when our agency office in Portland, Oregon landed the Amazon account in 1995. After a few meetings with Jeff Bezos, I started to understand what he was really building with all of his programmers. He was going to fundamentally change the way we shopped. I am not going to tell you that back then, I really understood the significant impact Amazon would have on the world of commerce. Our initial focus was to build the brand and sell books. And that's what we did. We did all the early research, brand strategy, creative design and built the core foundation for the Amazon brand. On purpose, we built a very powerful brand. Interestingly, a brand that only existed online. Amazingly, Amazon is now building retail stores. Geez, they just bought Whole Foods.

So with the rise of the Internet as a new medium, came a plethora of new "online" digital marketing agencies. While traditional advertising and marketing agencies largely ignored the Internet, these digital agencies grew rapidly and started to creep into more strategic marketing projects with larger brands. Time has marched on and now we are in a world where online marketing has become critical. With the rise of social media and customer reviews, being online is not a "nice to have" in marketing, it's a requirement and is now a core element of most brands' marketing strategy. So, if the traditional advertising agencies were laggards in embracing on-line marketing yet new online marketing shops are proliferating, who was training the new marketing leaders in these digital shops about marketing strategy and branding? No one. These digital agencies have grown so quickly that their leaders have never worked in an environment where they could learn or be trained about branding. As a matter of fact, you could have a 30-40 year old leader of a digital agency who has never worked on a "branding assignment" and now is responsible for perhaps leading a client's marketing efforts. Unless that leader has brought in other people who have had the brand strategy training, what do they think branding is? Online ads, videos, tweets, contests and promotions? Unfortunately, yes.

MARKETING WITHOUT BRANDING EXPERTISE, IS WELL, BULLST**

Going back to my lunch with the founder of the online marketing agency, he is not dumb. He is actually quite bright. He just does not understand the *craft* of building a brand. He does understand that brands always win over products but he simply does not know how to build a brand. He has never worked for a marketing Merlin. He has done what he has always done to help his online agency grow and thrive. Online tactical marketing. The only problem with understanding one medium "tactically" and not acquiring strategic marketing knowledge and expertise is that as you move upstream to work with larger clients and more powerful "brands" they all expect you to know marketing strategy and branding. It may not be exactly why they are hiring you but they expect you to know it. And if you don't know it, your tendency is to either "bullshit" your way through it or to actually offer recommendations that are really going to be based on bullshit. That is, you don't actually know what to do so you try and wing it. This is the most dangerous place to be as a marketer since you could damage your brand, the client business and definitely your career.

When you don't really understand the value or the creation of branding, you tend to do what you know, which is tactical product marketing. The only problem with that is that you will probably never construct the marketing needed to create a customer "feeling" which results in the customer viewing your product or service as valuable…until something better comes along. Let me give you an example. When GoPro launched, they did excellent product marketing and leveraged the customer's passion to create movies and photos and share them in social media. GoPro also benefited from the rapid and explosive growth in social media as a trend. So for almost 15 years, GoPro (founded in 2002) just kept improving the same core product, more or less, and never focused on diversifying the product line (strategy) or really building their brand value (i.e. software, helpful platform, etc.) So, where is GoPro today? Struggling. Not sure if they will survive. Quite frankly, do you love your GoPro?

Over time, brands that focus on the customer and stay relevant as a brand, meaning they continue to create a customer feeling that is uniquely positive, will thrive and continue to be leaders. Companies that focus on building great products but not great brands will face competition over time and ultimately struggle in the marketplace. They tend to focus on short terms results and do not take the long term view. Brands, not products, rule the marketplace.

WHAT'S IN IT FOR YOU SPECIFICALLY IN THIS BOOK?

Look, I am not bashing millennial marketers or entrepreneurs who are in rapidly growing companies. On the contrary, I want to help. I have been fortunate in my career to work with some amazing creatives, marketers and clients to create and grow some amazing brands. And while there are quite a few books on marketing strategy and branding, they are not complete, are one dimensional, lack detailed examples and don't deliver key insights from someone who has been there. If you asked me today, how many different books would you have to read to get a good understanding of marketing strategy and branding, I would be giving you a list of ten books to read. Instead of giving you that list, I am going to give you this one book. I will give you all of the insights and learnings that I have accumulated from all the great brands that I have worked with in the past. You will get the following: *An easy to understand overview of branding, ten brand building strategies, how branding trees, category ladders and repositioning works and a better understanding of the critical nature of brand positioning. In addition, I will explain how the four P's of marketing have changed and how you need to leverage an integrated brand marketing approach and how trends are shifting marketplace landscapes. I will also introduce tools like Blue Ocean strategy which can help you guide your brand or your clients brand to a better marketplace.*

Finally, throughout the book, at the end of each chapter, I will share with you my insights about several brands, why they succeeded or failed based on their branding and marketing strategies. All to help you better understand branding so that you can be more successful in your career. If you are ready to take this journey, then be my apprentice and I will be your Merlin. Then perhaps one day, with much work and practice, you will be someone's Merlin. If you really want to master branding, and not be in a place where you are relying on bullshit, then read on.

CHAPTER ONE
CUSTOMERS CAN FEEL BUT MARKETERS NEED TO SEE.
* * *

As a marketer today, your "marketing world" may be predominately digital with little exposure to marketing strategy or branding. You may be ten years into your career or you just entered the marketing world via online marketing and never had any strategic mentorship or training. As such, your marketing perspective and experience may be very tactical. Build a website. Run an AdWords campaign. Get that content up in social media. Run a contest or a promotion. All just digital marketing tactics. Have you ever taken the time to really get to know your potential end customer? Understand this: You are not the customer.

You can't assume you know what a customer wants or needs just because you are doing the marketing to attract that customer. Why do so many marketers assume they know what a customer wants or needs—even when those marketers themselves do not fit the target segment profile? And even if you do fit the target segment profile, don't assume you are the customer or know more than they do. You don't. You want to know why? You are not the customer. Ever meet a 45-year-old marketer who is marketing products for 18- to 25-year-old customers? Or the reverse? And, if you did, did you ever wonder what he or she was thinking?

Here is some advice for marketers: never assume you know your potential customer. Ever. That realization will force you to do several things:

- Always be researching the marketplace and trends
- Base your decisions about customers on as many **facts** as possible
- Surround yourself with other people who might have customer insights
- Relentlessly visit or understand the customer environment

Many digital marketers and company executives speak as though they are customer experts—yet where did they get that expertise? Do they have deep mentorship training on strategy and branding? Better yet, when did they transform themselves into the target customer?

Here is what you should do to learn more about your potential customers. Ask these types of questions:

What are the customers' ages, incomes, and sexes?

Where do they live?

What do they live in?

What kind of music do they listen to?

What kind of car do they drive? Lease or own?

Where do they shop for clothes?

What kind of food do they buy?

How do they use technology in their lives?

I could go on, but you get the point. You need to understand your customers. You can't assume that you know everything—or even anything — about them. You can't pretend that you are in the mindset of your customer. So, how do you find out more about your current or potential customers?

OBSERVATION LABS AND WALKING THE AISLES

What is the floor made of in an Apple Store? What color is it? Millions of people have walked into and on the floor in an Apple store yet cannot answer those two questions. Why? Often, as we move through life, we see but we do not observe. And to be a better marketer, you must learn to observe what goes on all around you. I spent 20 years in a marketing career working with some of the best brands in the world. My curiosity on "observing" in addition to reading marketing research reports came about because of my lack of understanding about my client's customers. So, I spent my entire career obsessing about learning more about potential customers than the competition or even my clients. And what I learned is that what you "see" is better than any research report.

Observational research or lab, ethnography, or, in plain English, "watching people do stuff," seems to make so much common sense but quite a few marketers just don't use it. You would think the largest brands in the world would use this everyday but they don't. Certainly, compared to traditional focus groups, mini-groups, or one-on-one interviews, observational research accounts for a pitiably small portion of most research budgets. Yogi Berra's famous line that "You can observe a lot just by watching" is widely acknowledged, but observation remains the most under-utilized qualitative technique in marketing research. One of the reasons seems to be that many clients (and researchers) just don't know how to get value out of simple observation. I have based my career on finding "customer truth" and I hunted it maniacally. What better "truth" than simply observing what is really happening?

The good news about conducting, designing or implementing an observation lab is that they are inexpensive, easy to do and anyone with the right mindset can do them. First, it's not about what you believe or know. It's not about your opinion. It's about getting answers to the types of questions listed below. Pretend you are the VP of Marketing for Whole Foods, perhaps a competitor, maybe even someone on their marketing agency team. We all know this grocery marketplace is becoming more competitive. What could be done differently? What could increase customer satisfaction or sales? How do we boost employee morale? Imagine you were visiting a

Whole Foods grocery store in the next few hours. One that you have been in 20 times before. This time, for the first time, you go to observe and answer these simple questions:

> What do you see?
>
> What do you smell?
>
> What do you hear?
>
> What are people doing?
>
> What is the "mood" of the place?
>
> Who is in the place?
>
> What is the purpose of the place?
>
> What color is the floor? The walls?
>
> What does this place make you "feel?
>
> What are you noticing for the first time?
>
> What is missing?
>
> Is this place busy? If so, why? If not, why?
>
> What are the descriptive words you would associate with this place?

For every observation lab, you could have an endless list of questions. Keep the questions simple and limit your questions to fewer than twenty. It's okay if you have an objective in mind but you need to keep your mind "open" or you will not really observe, you will just see what you want or expect to see. Here is the good news. If you have an open mind you will observe way more than you ever did before. Hopefully, all your senses, not just your eyes will be engaged.

Learning from watching is, in fact, hard. Since observation skills don't get sharpened up in real life the way questioning skills do, you need to train yourself to see, learn, and think when you watch people do what they do. It takes some practice, and some discipline. The one thing I have learned is to look for the ordinary, not the extraordinary.

When you first do an observation lab, people look like they aren't "doing" anything! They're just going about their business, and nothing that they're doing looks surprising. They're walking around at the mall, moving in and out of retail stores, buying their lunch in the food court. They're waiting for their cars to be serviced. Don't become alarmed. Slow down and just start taking real or mental notes of what you do see and hear even if nothing seems out of the ordinary. For example, when my students at San Diego State University did an observation lab at the campus bookstore, they thought "what would we really learn?" But they noticed simple things… like how people were queuing up in line across a main throughway to get to the main cash register or why certain products were not offered for sale or that there was a typo on a merchandising display. And so on. Ultimately they recorded 65 observations and based on a review, offered ten recommendations that we forwarded to the bookstore manager. He asked how we came up with five of the recommendations, which he said he would implement. We told him we spent 45 minutes in the bookstore and just observed.

Here are some simple guidelines that will help you with your own observation lab.

"ORDINARY" IS WHAT YOU'RE THERE TO OBSERVE. Don't go looking for something extraordinary. What you're really looking for are the insights hidden in "ordinary." Nothing people do is "natural". You may watch people walking into a retail environment. They'll walk in, look around to get their bearings, walk over to a display or proceed down an aisle, maybe pick up an item or two or compare prices. "Of course," you'll say to yourself, "that's just what I'd do in their shoes. It's just common sense." Observing what they really do is simply the first "truth" about what they really do. That's it.

WHATEVER YOU SAW COULD HAVE HAPPENED DIFFERENTLY. The retail store shoppers could have taken more time to get their bearings, or less time. They might have gone down a different aisle. They might have picked up more items, or not as many. They might have sought help from an employee. They might have, but they didn't. What they did needs to be explained. Start noticing the regularities: do most people need a period of time to get their bearings when they come into the store? Where are they when they do this? Where do they look? What do they see there? Is there something about the store environment that makes them do things the way they're doing them? Is the way they're behaving the optimum way you want your customers to behave? Look at the "rule breakers." Who are they? What regularities are they defying? Once you recognize that everything people do is the result of something, you can begin looking for that something. Maybe it's something about them. Or the people they're with. Or the environment

they're in. Find the simple something that makes people do what they do.

BECOME THE MASTER OF THE OBVIOUS. Take the most obvious thing you've observed. Maybe you were watching people wait to have their cars repaired, and they "didn't do anything." Maybe they actually fell asleep in the waiting area. Maybe they spent the whole time looking bored. Maybe they were on their smartphones. Ask yourself why they were so bored - and remember that boredom isn't natural. Humans are the most curious creatures on earth. The service waiting room had a TV, lots of magazines, today's newspaper, some sales material and several new car displays. Why didn't they get interested in any of that? Were they interested in anything? Not really - they'd get up, check on the progress of their cars, then sit down again. But maybe that's it: all they were interested in was their cars. They wanted to "see" what was happening with their cars! And that's all they wanted to see. How's that for obvious? What if your dealership had a second floor waiting room with a full wall of glass showing off the entire repair area? Would being able to see their cars being repaired make people less anxious and more satisfied?

SWEAT ALL THE LITTLE DETAILS. Take good notes. Make short movies. Think about where people walk, stand, sit, and look. For how long. Doing what. With whom. Note every little activity. Here's an example: Several years ago we were observing people using a newly designed gasoline pump. One of the first "pay at the pump" designs, it allowed drivers to insert a credit or ATM card so they could pay without having to walk to the cashier's station. We noticed a number of motorists driving up to the pump, getting out and looking at it, then climbing back into their cars, apparently searching for something. They'd get back out of the car, go back to the pump, and read the directions - which seemed to present some difficulty. At a certain point we began walking up to people and asked them what they were doing: "Looking for my reading glasses." In the haste to install the new pumps and print some simple directions, little attention was paid to the size and clarity of the typeface for the directions, which the energy company did not think people would need anyway. But since this was something new, they thought providing directions would be helpful. Would have been if it was easier to read. Better yet, why not design the pump interface so simply, you did not need directions.

THE "WHOLE ACTIVITY" IS THE KEY. Think of all of the customer's activities as concentric rings of context. Stopping for gas takes place inside the "driving somewhere" ring, which takes place inside the "going home from work" ring, and so forth. Most research projects involve single activity units like pumping gas, or kitchen cleanup, or visiting a fast-food drive-thru; but these aren't generally the whole activities. The whole activity is a set of behaviors that includes these small units plus at least one layer of context. It's "what's going on" from the consumer point of view, and it may be very different from what you think is actually happening. To get clues about a whole activity, look at how people enter the activity you're trying to observe, and how they exit. What's going on just before and just afterward? How do they get to the point you're interested in? What and who do they bring with them? Are they happy, sad or hurried? How do they leave? What do they take with them and what do they leave behind? If the concentric rings of customer activity are like a big multi-ringed bull's-eye, let the arrow find the target and not the other way around. You can do the same thing with an ecommerce brand if you "watch" visitor traffic in real time as they make their way through the website.

THE MOST OBVIOUS THINGS ARE OBVIOUS. The problem is that they are obvious in hindsight, and the context doesn't appear until it appears in a real observation. Want to hedge your observation bet? Marry your observation even more by watching and talking. My own feeling is that the deepest understanding of people comes from combining an analysis of what people do with an analysis of what people have to say. You can observe people all day long and you will get some insights. But combine observation with engaging with customers and asking them simple, non-leading questions. Why are you here today? Did you drive by yourself? Which route did you take? What are you shopping for today? Was there something you did not find? I have said it before and I will say it again. "Customers may not always be right but they are never wrong." Getting more insights from customers will help you with your product or brand strategy.

HOW DO YOU OBSERVE A DIGITAL BRAND?

If you are a digital marketer today, you probably are thinking that you can't do an observation lab on a "digital" company. Maybe you can. When we did all the initial branding and marketing for Amazon, we initially had no clue about what Amazon's brand promise should be, how that would come alive and how we could make the customers feel something powerful for an online only brand. So we spent time trying to understand who would be an influencer in the buying and recommending of books. That led us to about 1.3 million people in just New York, LA and San Francisco who were high income and thought leaders when it came to purchasing, consuming and recommending written content. Next we focused on the creation of the Amazon brand and how they would keep their brand promise. In order to do that we had to create a brand "persona" as if the brand were human. That led us to asking the question, "Who delights us?" For us it was boutique hotel concierges. So, we went and studied them more closely. Here is what we learned:

> How they greeted and welcomed people.
>
> That they remembered them.
>
> That they knew what returning guests wanted.
>
> That they would get things for guests.
>
> They would make recommendations.

Out of this brand persona research, we gave Jeff Bezos not only the core elements of the Amazon brand but also the brand attributes (e.g. one click login, reviews, recommendations, etc.) that you still see today. Later, we "observed" how a customer moved through the website through path analysis. Companies are being built today entirely in a digital world. Uber, AirBnb, SnapChat, etc. How long they thrive and survive is based on how powerful their brands become or stay relevant. What's key in their growth and survival is to really understand and create an emotional feeling with their target customers. If not, they will become a commodity which can be easily replaced.

WHAT A CUSTOMER FEELS IS CRITICAL

As a marketer, you usually have two choices in front of you with a marketing campaign or strategy: create something that is new and create a positive customer brand feeling or take an existing product or service and reinforce or change the customer brand feeling about that product or service. Most marketers do not understand that it is more important to understand what the customers "feel" than what the marketer "says." Nike can say, "Just do it" but they better make sure their customer internalizes that and "feels" like a champion when they are wearing Nike products or their message will fall flat.

So, how do you begin to understand what the customer is feeling right now? You need to be searching for customer "truth." Think relentless searching, which means "unending." Before you create your marketing or brand strategy, embrace the idea that you'll continually be in the customer's environment to learn about that customer. You're not just there at their purchase decision, but also wherever the actual customer environment is, whether that's a retail location, a dealership service area, a restaurant, a local mall, an airport, a grocery store or an ecommerce website. You will be studying customer behavior so well that you will "know" what they might do next. Additionally, you will need to study your competition and see how they treat their current customers, and what could possibly be improved. For example, as a general partner in our integrated marketing agency, CKS Partners ($1 billion agency with 10,000 employees), which dealt with creating new brands or launching new products, I regularly walked into the customer environment and met with real customers. I never relied exclusively on surveys, research data or third-party industry reports. I needed to "feel and touch" the customers. I needed to see what they felt, to better understand their patterns, to really get insights into the trends that were affecting them or those that were potentially starting As a marketer, you need to be zealous in your approach to understanding your current or potential customers. Just as an aside, it would have helped Blockbuster Video and Borders Books if they had watched or listened to their customers!

You may or may not believe that a customer's "feelings" about the brand you are working with matters. But you need to believe this: customers

CUSTOMERS CAN FEEL BUT MARKETERS NEED TO SEE.

may not always know what they want, but they are never wrong. So, you need to be constantly learning what customers are feeling in order to understand what messages you need to reinforce or create in your marketing strategy. How important is understanding or creating a powerful "emotional" connection to your customers? Research conducted by several firms across hundreds of brands in dozens of categories shows that the most effective way to maximize customer value is to move beyond mere customer satisfaction and connect with customers at an emotional level – tapping into their fundamental motivations and fulfilling their deep, often unspoken emotional needs. That means appealing to any of dozens of "emotional motivators" such as a desire to feel a sense of belonging, to succeed in life, or to feel secure. On a lifetime value basis, emotionally connected customers are more than **twice as valuable** as highly satisfied customers. These emotionally connected customers buy more of your products and services, visit you more often, exhibit less price sensitivity, pay more attention to your communications, follow your advice, and recommend you more. That is why you want to really understand what a customer feels. But how do you create that customer feeling for your brand?

ARCHITECTING THE CUSTOMER FEELING

As a marketer, you may have the ambition of moving up your career ladder and being someone who can create a brand so powerful that it emotionally connects its customers and produces a powerful set of customer feelings. Ever walk past someone sitting at a restaurant table or attending a networking event and they say to the person next to them," I love my iPhone." Did you ever stop to think about their comment? Love their iPhone? Is that comment an accident? No, it's not. It's exactly what Apple and Steve Jobs intended. So, how do you architect a marketing strategy and set of tactics to create a powerful feeling that a customer believes in and will say out loud?

AIM FOR YOUR CUSTOMERS' HEARTS, NOT THEIR WALLETS

There's a big difference between sticking with a brand and being stuck with one. If your customers aren't happy with your brand but they stay with you because of hefty switching costs, they're not sticking with you—they're stuck with you. Nobody wants to be held prisoner, so if your company's customer-retention strategy relies on making it difficult for people to leave, you're not building brand loyalty—and you're not building a great brand. To create valuable, sustainable customer relationships, great brands don't sell customers on contracts—they seduce them with emotional connections. Impactful, memorable, emotional connections lead to true brand loyalty.

Consider Virgin America's appeal. Virgin provides luxurious interiors, in-flight wi-fi, live TV and on-demand food service. Its fleet is 25 percent more carbon-efficient than the U.S. average and the company reduces its footprint with progressive practices like single-engine taxiing, idle reverse landings and regulated cruising speed. Customers themselves can even make a difference in-flight by purchasing carbon offsets or making a charitable donation through Virgin's entertainment system.

But these features aren't why customers want to fly with Virgin again and again. The reason is that Virgin treats its customers like special guests, tending to their needs and making sure they're comfortable and content. The company's stated goal is "to always provide you with an unforgettable experience that adds value to your trip." To that end, its staff is empowered to make decisions on the spot to help customers. This level of care and attention has established Virgin as a brand that takes care of its customers and cares about the planet. And this has inspired fierce loyalty, with many brand loyal fans going out of their way to fly Virgin. By consistently executing on its brand values, Virgin employees give customers every reason to love flying with them. Once you've had the best flight of your life, it's hard to settle for what other airlines offer, even if you've racked up their frequent-flier miles or are tied to one of their credit cards.

People decide which brands to buy and which ones to stick with based on how the brands make them feel. That's why great brands aren't in the business of selling products—they're in the business of forging close emotional ties with their customers.

So, it's important for you as a marketer to understand how to create emotional customer connections in order to create powerful brand "feelings" that are internalized by your customers. Do that and you will have created a powerful brand. Here are four insights to help you craft a brand from an emotional customer perspective:

1. Ground your brand identity **in emotional values** that set you apart from the competition and resonate with your consumers. Product features and claims of efficacy should be used only to support those values.

2. Give **long-term customer relationships** priority over short-term sales. While this is a widely accepted notion, the pressure to demonstrate immediate return on investment and the traditional managerial imperative to reach for top-line revenue goals lead companies to put sales ahead of relationships. Leaders need to resist the urge to chase the sale, and their best defense is a firm commitment to their brand identity (see above).

3. Use your brand—**not product categories**—to determine your business scope and scale. Your focus on creating deeper emotional bonds with customers should drive future product innovations and brand extensions. Dollar Shave Club started by selling razors to young men; now they sell grooming kits via their subscription business model.

4. Perpetually ask and answer: **"What business are we really in?"** Virgin America isn't in the business of selling flights. Its business is making good friends during relaxing, luxurious, and affordable experiences. With this level of commitment to making an emotional connection, Virgin, like other great brands, continuously redefines consumer expectations and challenges the norms of its industry categories.

Most brands have the same business goals as most companies do: long-term customer loyalty, retention, and satisfaction that generate a continuing revenue stream from existing customers. But great brands achieve their goals by forging personal and meaningful bonds with customers. An emotional connection is what separates brands from companies that are just selling products. And customers are able to tell the difference.

HOW CUSTOMERS RATIONALIZE BRANDS

Not all brands are created equal no matter how successful they are. When we need a tissue, we ask for a Kleenex. That does not mean we actually value the brand Kleenex. In fact we just need a tissue. The same goes for making copies on a copier. Give me a Xerox means, make me a copy. Not necessarily on a Xerox copier but on any copier. In that same manner of thinking, customers have a hierarchy of how they perceive brands in their minds and hearts. Some brands are transactional, others vie to meet their specific needs and the best brands are those which the customer believes have no substitute. Here is the simple hierarchy in a customer's mind:

BRAND RATIONALE HIERARCHY

1. *JUST **MEET** MY NEEDS.* In any customer experience there are a set of needs that the customer is trying to satisfy. The lowest level of the brand hierarchy is simply about whether or not these needs were met by the brand. For example, if a customer goes to a store to buy a product and it's out of stock then they will buy whatever product is there that also meets their needs. Think ant spray, paper towels, cooking oil, etc. It's very hard to make one of these brands standout unless it has a specific attribute or benefit that no other product has in that category.

2. *YOU HAVE TO **SATISFY** MY NEEDS.* The middle level of the hierarchy is about how easy it was for the customer to have their needs satisfied. This is all about the effort that they need to expend getting what they want. A great experience in a customer's eyes is getting what they want with the least possible amount of effort. Minimizing physical movement, searching time or making relevant comparisons easy are all example of reducing effort for the customer. Understand though that simply satisfying the customer does not mean that they are loyal to your brand. They might buy the BMW this time but if Audi comes out with a killer design and the same performance specs, they might be gone.

3. *YOU BETTER **DELIGHT** ME.* The final and top-most level of the hierarchy is all about enjoyment and creating the most powerful feeling

CUSTOMERS CAN FEEL BUT MARKETERS NEED TO SEE.

a customer will have regarding products in that category. If you can make the customer actually enjoy the experience on an emotional level, rather than the more functional dimensions that are lower down the hierarchy then, and only then, will you have a chance of gaining a brand advocate. Customers will believe there is no substitute for your product or service. They will say this: "I love my iPhone." "I start every day of my life with a Starbucks." "When I run in my Nike's, it's like I am floating."

Creating brands seems like it would be easy but it's hard. What are you selling, a brand or a product? Last year, more than 250,000 new products were launched on a worldwide basis. According to a Harvard Business Review study, 95% of them will fail. In order to increase your odds of success, you better understand core branding basics which will be covered in the next chapter.

BRAND INSIGHT

In 1996, our agency office in Portland, Oregon was in the middle of launching a new brand and in order to get more insights from potential partners, competitors and industry experts, I attended a major trade show event. The goal was to get more information that would help us with our new client. This event was huge representing an industry with more than $21.3 billion in annual sales. The first day was a blur, listening to speakers and wandering a large trade show floor with hundreds of companies in various sized booths. On the morning of the second day, I walked up to a coffee kiosk and ordered a hot tea. A man walked up and ordered a coffee. The way he was standing, I could not see his name badge. Making small talk, I asked him how the trade show was going for him. He replied that it was fine. Curiously, I thought I would ask him what he thought about Amazon, the new Internet upstart in this major book industry. He replied, "Amazon's sales will never amount to much and people will just never buy things on the Internet. We are building new 25,000 square foot stores with coffee bars and music CD's and that is exactly what our customers want." I saw his name badge as he turned and walked away. Boy, I thought, the CEO of Borders just does not get it. Amazon is not trying to sell books online. They are trying to build a brand to delight customers so that one day, customers will order everything from them.

KEY TAKEAWAY

From the very first meeting with Jeff Bezos, he made it very clear that the brand he wanted us to build would leverage a coming massive trend to buy things online. That is why we never positioned Amazon against Borders or Barnes & Noble in our early marketing campaigns. They were not the long term competition. Know the brand you are building and what you are really selling. Better yet, follow trends and know what customers really need.

CUSTOMERS CAN FEEL BUT MARKETERS NEED TO SEE.

CHAPTER TWO
BRANDING 101: AN OVERVIEW.
* * *

The word "branding" can mean different things to different people. But for marketers, it should only mean one thing. Let's look at the definition of branding.

> *Branding is the process involved in creating a unique name and image for a product in the* **consumers' mind,** *mainly through marketing campaigns with a consistent theme and messaging. Branding aims to establish a significant and differentiated presence in the market that attracts and retains loyal customers.*

Well if that is the definition, why are there so many interpretations of branding? Because 9 out of 10 digital marketers I meet today simply do not understand branding at all. Mixing up marketing and branding is only one of the most common misconceptions about branding that you will encounter. Many businesses and marketers handling branding tasks have the following misconceptions:

MISCONCEPTION #1: Branding is marketing / advertising / promotion / anything to that effect. This is a misconception because branding goes deeper than marketing. Marketing, advertising, and other promotional activities only *communicate* your brand personality and message. Your brand is comprised of your personality, your voice, and your message; branding is the process of establishing these traits.

MISCONCEPTION #2: You are the ultimate authority when it comes to your brand. This is a very common misconception, especially among first-time marketers and business owners. The truth is while you set the tone and get the ball rolling so to speak, and you set the guidelines that your organization will follow and live by as regards your brand, this does not automatically make you the ultimate brand authority. Your customers are the ones who ultimately define your brand. Their *perception* of your brand is what sticks with the people they influence. This is why it's very important to select your brand values carefully; otherwise, your brand may be taken the wrong way – or worse, it may fail when you don't see repeat customers.

MISCONCEPTION #3: There must be a formula for success when it comes to branding. Just because everything in online marketing can be measured doesn't mean everything has a formula. No two companies are alike. While a similar process for developing a brand may work for businesses in the same field, for example, these businesses will still have unique identities and needs. The truth is that there is no formula – branding is and will always be a customized experience. The good news is you can measure the success of your brand easily. What you should look at in this case is the behavior and the interests of your target audience. You can measure initial sales and you can measure brand loyalty and repeat sales.

With all these misconceptions about branding, it's no wonder that in the absence of knowledge, training and mentorship, most digital marketers rely on the communication of "bullshit" to drive their marketing campaigns.

BRANDING ≠ BULLSHIT: WHY BRANDING SHOULD MATTER TO DIGITAL MARKETERS

Whether you know it or not, you have a brand. Every interaction you've had with your customers and every one of the 140 characters you've sent out on Twitter has worked to develop your brand. These interactions, although seemingly small and unrelated, collectively form the basis of your relationship with your audience, and all relationships are facilitated, maintained and articulated by—none other than—your brand.

Meaning, your brand is already alive. And if you aren't being intentional about it, it can quickly grow to be a disorderly, uncontrollable and wild force happening in the marketplace. That's what can make branding such a hard process to understand. Branding is indeed an intricate and involved process. The first step is to understand why branding matters.

WHAT IS BRANDING? A WORKING DEFINITION OF BRAND.
The best place to start is to understand what a brand isn't. Your brand isn't your logo. Your brand isn't your visual identity system or your retina-ready website. It isn't your color scheme or even your wonderful product. And most importantly, your brand isn't what you say it is. Your brand is what they say it is. They meaning people, people meaning humans and humans meaning the intuitive, flawed and emotive beings we all are. In other words, your brand is a "gut feeling" that's rooted deep within people. It's a personal feeling because brands are defined by individuals, one by one, human by human. And when enough individuals arrive at the same gut feeling, we have a brand.

BRANDING ≠ BULLSHIT. Many marketers equate branding to excess, prodigality and even bullshit. It's the notion that branding is just the stupefying marketing noise (sizzle) that sells the real thing (the steak). This notion is fueled by the belief that features, benefits and the "x factor" of a new product alone create value and, therefore, there is no need to spend already scarce time working on brand development instead of product development. Yet the single most challenging hurdle facing a marketer is just as real as the others. Product marketing is easy, building a brand is hard. But having a differentiated brand could make all the difference in the success of the product.

BRAND SIMPLIFIES CHOICE. It is the simplest to understand: People have too many choices and too little time. A byproduct of our over-messaged and hyper-connected culture is the proliferation of choice. Consider the toothpaste aisle alone. There are over 400 different types and brands of toothpaste to choose from. Some whiten, some are meant for sensitive teeth, some are dentist-approved and some are even gluten free and organic. Add in the thousands of choices for what type of toothbrush you're going to use to apply your toothpaste and the simple act of brushing your teeth can become an overwhelming myriad of choice. If just brushing your teeth presents a person with an immense amount of choice, what about the rest of the marketplace? A powerful brand has the ability to stand out where it matters most. In the customers mind.

I know what you're thinking, "That might be true, but our product is so unique, so different, we'll be the only one out there." I hate to say it, but that's probably not reality. If you are one of the very, very few marketers who are marketing something so unique and different that there is literally no basis for comparison, kudos to you. For the rest of us, we will face the challenge of over-saturated choice sooner rather than later. That's where the brand proves itself as the opposite of excess, prodigality and bullshit. Why? Because the brand simplifies our choice. People, as emotional, intuitive beings, base their buying decisions on trust. Trust is gained from the relationships developed between people and organizations, and that relationship is facilitated by your brand. Very simply: Brand ≠ Bullshit; Brand = Relationship. To take it a step further: Brand = Relationship = Trust = Value. If you can help the customer internalize the "value" of your product and create that powerful customer feeling that there is no replacement for your brand, then you are well on your way to building an amazing brand. In order to better understand branding, let's go back to the beginning of branding.

THE HISTORY OF BRANDING

The concept of branding has been around for hundreds of years and likely much longer. What it means to brand something has broadened quite a bit since the word first came into use. Despite the changes, each of the older kinds of branding is still in wide use today. The modern word "brand" is derived from the word "Brandr", a word from Ancient Norse meaning "to burn". Around 950 A.D. a "brand" referred to a burning piece of wood. By the 1300s it was used primarily to describe a torch, essentially a burning piece of wood that was used as a tool. By the 1500s the meaning had changed to refer to a mark burned on cattle to show ownership. Individual ranches would each have their own unique mark so ownership could be determined if their animals were lost, stolen, or mixed in with animals from another ranch. Each brand had to be simple, unique, and easy to identify quickly – essential traits that are still common to modern logos.

The 1820's saw the rise of the mass production and shipment of trade goods. As products like ale and wine were produced in larger batches and wider distribution, manufacturers began burning their "mark" onto crates and cases of goods to distinguish themselves from their competition. Over time, the brand evolved into a symbol of quality rather than ownership. Products that were perceived as having a high and consistent quality could command a higher price than their undistinguished alternatives. In 1870, it became possible to register a trademark to prevent competitors from creating confusingly similar products. Brands promised functional benefits such as Coca Cola's 1905 slogan, "*Coca Cola Revives and Sustains.*" Brands themselves were becoming more valuable than the actual product.

The introduction of radio and television gave manufacturers new ways to create demand for their products. In 1928, Edward Bernays, the nephew of Sigmund Freud, published a book called Propaganda. Bernays argued that by associating products with ideas large numbers of people could be persuaded to change their behavior. The book was enormously popular, and advertising agencies on Madison Avenue took notice. By the 1960's, marketers were using mass media to associate brands with emotional benefits rather than functional ones. Advertisements showed how using a particular brand would make you more desirable, part of an exclusive club, or — as Coca Cola promised in 1979 with "*Have a Coke and a Smile!*" — just happier.

By the 1980's, distribution channels reached around the globe and consumers had more choices than ever. Companies began to focus on building brand recognition for themselves rather than focusing exclusively on their products and services. This allowed them to build brand loyalty that extended across product lines and gave their consumers a sense of belonging and personal meaning. In 1984, Apple Computer released their iconic "1984" television ad that showed users breaking free of rigid conformity by using Apple computers. The computer itself was almost an afterthought in this powerful ad. Branding became strategic and took off;

businesses began to focus on establishing long term corporate identity rather than creating short ad campaigns. Advertising agencies grew into brand consultancies. Corporate branding extended to non-profits, political groups, and even personal brands for celebrities.

The rise of the internet and social media is driving the next stage in the evolution of branding. Unlike consumers of the past, internet-connected people of today aren't satisfied to merely consume – they want to participate. Social media brands like YouTube and Facebook rely on their users to help establish their value and how they are perceived by the public. Content sites like Amazon and Yelp depend on reviewers to provide their most persuasive content. Although internet-based companies give up some of the control of their brand image, the loyalty from an actively participating customer base is unparalleled. Viral marketing, search engine optimization, and outsourced delivery allow organizations to gain visibility and deliver products without spending millions on advertising and infrastructure. So today, it is possible to create a brand, have no physical presence and have people around the world believe your brand is just as good if not better than the physical representation of brand. Amazon versus Walmart. Think retail and the destruction that is occurring in that marketplace with online retailers beginning to decimate actual retail brands with physical stores. Food delivery service brands are becoming more important than the actual food. We are indeed entering an interesting era and there is no better time to understand branding and to become a brand expert.

THE MAKING OF A BRAND EXPERT

Are people born to be marketers? Do brand experts just rise from among the sea of marketers? Becoming an expert in anything does not just happen. It takes focus, purpose and years of practice. Researchers and educators have studied exactly how some people become experts. And guess what? It does not happen overnight.

Thirty years ago, two Hungarian educators, László and Klara Polgár, decided to challenge the popular assumption that women just don't succeed in areas requiring spatial thinking, such as chess. They wanted to make a point about the power of education. The Polgárs homeschooled their three daughters, and as part of their education the girls started playing chess with their parents at a very young age. Their systematic training and daily practice paid off. By 2000, all three daughters had been ranked in the top ten female players in the world. The youngest, Judit, had become a grand master at age 15, breaking the previous record for the youngest person to earn that title, held by Bobby Fischer, by a month. Judit became one of the world's top players and has defeated almost all the best male players.

It's not only assumptions about gender differences in expertise that have started to crumble. Back in 1985, Benjamin Bloom, a professor of education at the University of Chicago, published a landmark book, Developing Talent in Young People, which examined the critical factors that contribute to talent. He took a deep retrospective look at the childhoods of 120 elite performers who had won international competitions or awards in fields ranging from music and the arts to mathematics and neurology. Surprisingly, Bloom's work found no early indicators that could have predicted the virtuosos' success. Subsequent research indicating that there is no correlation between IQ and expert performance in fields such as chess, music, sports, and medicine has borne out his findings.

So what does correlate with success? One thing emerges very clearly from Bloom's work: All the superb performers he investigated had practiced intensively, had studied with devoted teachers, and had been supported enthusiastically by their families throughout their developing years. Later research building on Bloom's pioneering study revealed that the amount and quality of practice were key factors in the level of expertise people achieved. Consistently and overwhelmingly, the evidence showed that *experts are always made, not born.* These conclusions are based on rigorous research that looked at exceptional performance using scientific methods that are verifiable and reproducible. Most of these studies were compiled in The Cambridge Handbook of Expertise and Expert Performance, published by Cambridge University Press and edited by K. Anders Ericsson, one of the authors of this article. The 900-page-plus handbook includes contributions from more than 100 leading scientists who have studied expertise and top performance in a wide variety of domains:

surgery, acting, chess, writing, computer programming, ballet, music, aviation, firefighting, and many others. In other words, a lot of smart people have studied "expertise" and concluded it can be learned.

The journey to truly superior performance is neither for the faint of heart nor for the impatient. The development of genuine expertise requires struggle, sacrifice, honesty, and often painful self-assessment. There are no shortcuts. It will take you at least a decade to achieve expertise, and you will need to invest that time wisely. Here are three pieces of advice on how to potentially become a brand expert on purpose:

ACQUIRE BRAND KNOWLEDGE. When was the last time you read articles, studies or even a book on branding other than this book? How are you going to learn to "cook" if you don't get in the kitchen? Set up Google Alerts on branding, read several books on branding (will provide a list later in the book), attend workshops on branding and maybe even take a branding class at a local university.

ENGAGING IN "DELIBERATE" PRACTICE. You are not going to become a brand expert if you don't practice the art of branding. Quite a bit of this practice should focus on tasks beyond your current level of competence and comfort. Do a brand analysis. Create a branding tree. Go to a workshop on branding and really participate. Put yourself out there. Don't try and fool people either. Let them know you are a marketer who wants to learn the art of branding. They will help you if you are authentic and don't try and bullshit them.

YOU WILL NEED A WELL-INFORMED COACH. Everyone needs a coach or mentor in their professional life. In this case you need to find someone who can really help you understand what you don't know about branding. And this person needs to be a "brand expert". Take the time to seek out this person as there are not many of them in any marketplace who are truly experts. Look for people who have actually built or managed brands.

BE PATIENT, IT TAKES TIME. If you want to achieve top performance as a brand expert, you've got to forget the folklore about genius that makes many people think they cannot take a scientific approach to developing expertise. Experts are not born, they are made. It's going to take you between five and seven years to become an expert who is really knowledgeable and good.

RUN WITH A PACK. There is nothing like a "pack" mentality to learn even more and perhaps a bit faster. In my marketing career, I had an amazing mentor who taught me about branding. But what accelerated that learning was hanging out with other marketing professionals who were also learning the art of marketing and branding. It was not long before I had surrounded myself with other people my age who were smarter than me and we all shared points of view and knowledge we were learning. It might have been over beers or even a ballgame. But I learned a lot from my peers who I respected. I got to practice via our conversations and fuel my learning about branding.

CRAFTING A BRAND PROMISE

It's critical to every brand that they have an underlying "promise" that they are making to their customers. And if you are a great brand the promise is never said or appears in any of the marketing communications. It is "felt" by the customer who has internalized all the marketing messages and believes in your promise. Let me give you an example via Nike. Nike is meticulous about their marketing, their brand image, their endorsements of top athletes, etc. All to support their tagline of "Just do it." But that only serves to deliver their unwritten promise and that is, "If you wear or use Nike products, you will have the opportunity to be a champion." That is what customers "feel" from Nike. It's how Nike has built a multi-billion brand that can with stand the test of time and competitors. Here are some guidelines in building a brand promise:

Simple is better. It should be no longer than a simple sentence or two. A brand promise is not the same thing as a mission statement, which can often get convoluted with rambling sentences. An effective brand promise combines the catchiness of a tagline and reinforces it with the essence of the company's mission. However, it's not the tagline. Credibility is key. If the customer experience doesn't match the brand promise, the value of your brand is weakened. An example of a brand promise not living up to expectations comes from Ford Motor Company. During the 1980s, Ford's brand tagline was, "Quality is Job 1." However, owners of Ford's vehicles were not impressed as their vehicles routinely broke down. It got so bad that consumers gave Ford their own version of a brand promise: "Ford – Found On Roadside Broken."

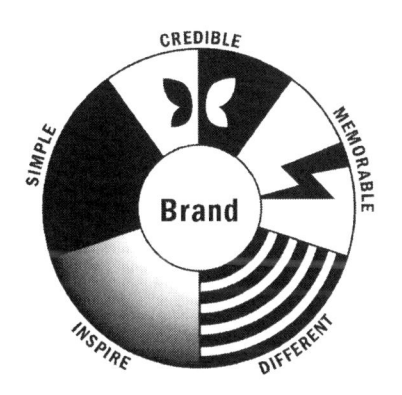

BRAND PROMISE

Better be different. If your brand promise sounds similar to other brand promises, especially a competitor's, how can you distinguish yourself from the pack? You need to discover what makes your company unique and different from your competitors. This goes beyond the features and benefits of your product and straight to the soul of your company and heart of your employees.

Has to be memorable. A brand promise should impact every decision your company makes. While a promise may not be as catchy as a tagline or slogan, it must be memorable enough for employees to embrace it and use it during customer interactions. And, in turn, it is then internalized by the customers who just feel your brand has no easy substitute.

Inspire People. People, in general, will act when they feel an emotional connection to a person or a product or a company. An effective brand promise helps establish that connection by being inspiring. At the same time, don't promise what you can't deliver. A brand promise is meant to inspire, but you also want to be realistic. A great example of an inspirational brand promise was Apple's "Think Different" campaign. It promised amazing hardware and software that would allow you to do your very best work.

THE CORE ELEMENTS OF A BRAND

If you are going to build a brand or even revitalize one, you need to be aware and understand the core elements that go into crafting a brand. Here are the core elements I look to create in a brand:

CORE BRAND ELEMENTS

1. *BRAND IDENTITY.* The brand of course is an easily recognizable name that immediately tells people about a certain organization that manufactures certain products or delivers certain services. Brand identity is the way people recognize the brand. It may be through the logo or other associated visuals. The Apple logo is very simple but it is immediately recognizable worldwide.

2. *BRAND IMAGE.* Brand image is the idea of the brand that people develop in their minds. It also dictates what they expect, and don't expect, from the brand. For instance, Mercedes has the image of a luxury car maker. So, it cannot be building a budget car even if there was a large market. Its existing premium customers won't take to it kindly as it dilutes the current image. Actually, Mercedes has done just that but not under their brand name. The Smart Car has its own brand and is not directly associated with Mercedes in the USA.

It's hard and sometimes impossible to change a brand image so it's best to know what you're aiming at before you invest hard earned dollars.

3. *BRAND POSITIONING.* Positioning is the way a product is placed in the market and in the customers mind. It basically defines what segments of the market the brand is targeting. For instance, Patagonia is a brand targeted at outdoor enthusiasts and experts. Basic ingredients in all outdoor gear might be similar but this one has been positioned to attract its customers with its expert focus on design, functionality and sustainability. Who does not want to wear Patagonia?

4. *BRAND PERSONALITY.* Brand personality is just like the personality of human beings. It is certain emotional or personal qualities that we associate with a particular brand. For example, we can associate youthfulness with Pepsi or ruggedness with Dewalt tools. Every single element of the brand identity including the color of the logo and the typography on the brand name adds to the personality.

5. *BRAND EQUITY.* Brand equity is the value of a brand. It may include tangible financial value such as market share and revenue as well as intangible aspects such as strategic benefits of the brand. For example Apple is a major technology brand and people perceive it is a premium, cutting edge manufacturer of quality products. So, it is not only the sales but the sheer image that takes the brand equity to a different level altogether.

6. *BRAND EXPERIENCE.* Brand experience is a combination of everything that a customer goes through while purchasing and using that brand. For example how does one feel while ordering food and eating at KFC? How does the staff behave and how fast do they deliver the food, and of course how did the food taste? Also, since it has many stores all over the world, customers expect all of them to maintain uniform standards of brand experience.

7. *BRAND DIFFERENTIATION.* Differentiation, as the word suggests is how a brand stands out in the crowd. For instance Dell

Computers lets people choose their components and assemble their own computer system, thus making it different from others who just sell readymade computers at retail stores with no scope for customization.

8. *BRAND COMMUNICATION.* Brand communication is the core message that is delivered through various media sources like advertising, brochures, online marketing, trade shows, packaging, etc. If the brand has to grow, it must be able to clearly communicate its core benefits to its customers. Consistently across all media.

9. *BRAND GAP.* Brand gap is the difference between what a brand promises to deliver in its communications and what it actually does. For its own sake, the gap should not be very large at all. A successful brand must be able to deliver what it promises. By the way, no amount of advertising or content marketing efforts can save a bad product or weak service.

10. *BRAND EXTENSION.* Brand extension is basically the idea of going beyond ones original products and services and exploring newer fields. For example Google started as a search engine. But now it provides many other services including email, adwords advertising and a mobile operating system called Android. This is how it has extended the brand but it must be done in a manner so that the existing brand equity complements the newer initiatives. Google's great brand equity was acquired through its stellar search operations and this is what enabled it to develop other services related to its core brand.

If creating a brand today takes expertise, knowledge of the marketplace, understanding the completion and the customers, what happens when you accelerate everything? Markets are being created or disrupted so quickly today that it is very challenging for marketers. With this increased speed, you do need to act or react but how you do it, not how fast you do it, is what will determine if you overcome the challenges facing you and your brand.

BRAND INSIGHT

This brand was first created in 1888. Yes, 1888. They were pioneers with their technology which involved the early creation of photographic cameras that were inexpensive. Over the years, they became experts on the innovation of film and even sophisticated x-ray technology. Then in the early 1990's, they actually invented the ability to take a digital photograph. Their products and technology were utilized in virtually every camera in the marketplace. While they were certainly market leaders in photo technology, they completely misread the photography marketplace as digital photos exploded. First with digital cameras and obviously now with Smartphones. The world did not stop taking photos. The amount of photos taken in the world keeps increasing especially with the rise of social media. Somehow this multi-billion brand missed all of that. And so Kodak, the brand which once owned the very "thought" of photography went away.

KEY TAKEAWAY

Customers did not want to take film-based analog photos anymore. They want to take digital photos. Kodak should have adapted and become a version of Flickr or better yet, have embraced digital photography as a medium and created or bought Instagram or even Snapchat. The world is constantly changing and relevant brands need to adapt in order to survive. If customers don't "feel" you anymore, you will go away.

CHAPTER THREE
THE CHALLENGE OF BRANDING TODAY.
* * *

The challenge of branding today is that it is very easy for someone to create a logo. As a matter of a fact almost anyone can create a logo. There are online crowd based websites, where for $5 to $99, designers from all over the world will create a logo. And then some executive or marketer from that company will slap that logo on the website and launch the company. However, that does not even come close to creating a brand. What is the brand meaning behind the logo? What does it begin to stand for in the marketplace? How is the product or service differentiation reflected in the brand? What do we want the customer to feel? You can't create a logo for a company and think that you are creating a brand. You need to do your homework, understand the marketplace and trends, understand your competition and most important, understand your potential customers.

CUSTOMERS ARE NOT ALWAYS RIGHT, BUT THEY ARE NEVER WRONG

I have met thousands of customers in my career and you know what, I never get tired of meeting them. And neither should you. Today, my customers are college students who are taking my creativity and entrepreneurship courses and participating in the Lavin Entrepreneurship Center programs. I get constant feedback through interactions in the classroom and through student surveys. The survey feedback has both quantitative scores and qualitative comments. I read everything. I look for little aha's—

those comments that point toward ways to improve my courses. Just when I think I have created the world's best entrepreneurship course, a student comment will let me know that I have yards to go. Even though we know we really need it, sometimes "customer truth" is hard to accept. And yet this truth yields incredible customer insights.

Customer truth is the heart of understanding exactly what kind of brand to create. There is a logical reason for this. As a marketer, your biggest ally is your customer.

If you connect with your customers and keep your brand promise, those customers will help you with your marketing. They will write solid reviews. Via word of mouth, they will tell others about your product or service. But ignore them and you do so at your peril. A great brand strategy that's poorly executed with customers is in real trouble. Especially if those customers have the option to buy a similar type of product or service from your competitors. A service company I consulted with recently was revisiting its brand and marketing strategy. I asked the employees to name a company they admired for its customer service but that they had never met an employee of that company. They were puzzled for a few minutes. Then one person said, "Amazon." I asked why. The person said, "They keep their promise." The rest of the employees in the room murmured their agrement.

In your lifetime, you may not ever meet an Amazon employee face to face. So why is this "brand" so successful? Because "they" never stop responding to their customers' needs. In 1996, when Jeff Bezos asked our agency to handle all of Amazon's initial branding and marketing, we spent months trying to figure out how to differentiate this "brand" from its competitors. We didn't even work on any creative elements for the first three months. Instead, we focused on the customers, on their expectations and what would delight them. Our agency team was stalled in some initial brainstorming, so we asked ourselves, "Who delights us with service?" After some discussion, we all agreed it was boutique hotel concierges. So we went out in Portland and Seattle and visited them. We saw how these concierges remembered and greeted people who came back repeatedly to stay with them. How they provided reviews and recommendations for local restaurants. How they retrieved newspapers for guests. How they asked people if they enjoyed their stay. This "concierge mentality" was designed into the Amazon experience that you still see today based on a branding strategy created in1996. And if the branding is done well, it could be timeless. Seek customer truth so that you discover how to delight your customers.

MARKETPLACE CREATION AND DISRUPTION

In the world we live in today, everything seems to be moving so fast. Products and services seem to be falling from the sky. Maybe one day they will. It used to be that marketplaces formed over longer periods of time. Not anymore. Uber was not here yesterday, here today. And that company creation spawned a number of companies moving into and growing that marketplace. Is it a product or brand race? Time will tell but the good news is, that if you are a marketer, you can take advantage of marketplaces that used to be difficult or expensive to enter. You just need to notice a customer trend shifting in the marketplace and create a brand to meet a new or expanding need. I could buy pet food at the store. Or I could have it delivered by a new brand to the house via a subscription model. Same $24 billion industry. Tremendous opportunities for marketers to architect new brands and create or disrupt large marketplaces. But you have to really understand the marketplace and know what kind of brand will capture your potential customer's hearts.

I network with quite a few online marketers. So, I get to hear lots of interesting ideas. These marketers are pitching me all time about brands they want to create, launch or even to discuss the brand they work at today. For a brand strategy to work, you need to have identified the initial niche segment of your target market that would care about your product or service. And honestly, the marketplace itself should hopefully be potentially large. I am a big fan of large, emerging, or disrupted marketplaces. The notion that marketers just need to come up with new ideas to drive the marketing for a successful company may work sometimes but I have learned that it's the marketplace that matters most. You can have an amazing brand or market strategy, but if there is no clear market opportunity, it might just as well be worthless. Remember: big marketplace, big opportunity. So when you think of a potentially great product or service, or perhaps a solution to a current problem, put that idea into an existing marketplace. And then ask yourself some simple questions:

> Is this a large marketplace?
>
> Is the market easily defined?
>
> Can I reach people in the marketplace easily?
>
> Is the market growing?
>
> Is the marketplace being disrupted?
>
> Is the marketplace fragmented?
>
> Who are the competitors?
>
> Who is the top competitor?
>
> What frustrates customers?
>
> What are customers valuing?
>
> Are customers' needs changing?
>
> What brand strategy allows me to be the leader?

You really can't put together a brand or marketing strategy on any product or service unless you understand the marketplace and its potential customers. The more you examine that potential marketplace, the more likely you will then spot something that you can really investigate. Just remember, if you have a large opportunity, going back to the beginning of the chapter, creating a logo or doing some tactical digital marketing does not create a brand.

DON'T MAKE THESE TEN DIGITAL MARKETING MISTAKES

In the age of marketing, digital marketing is still relatively new and emerging however companies in many industries recognize the importance and impact of this new medium on their brands. From smartphones to social media, digital marketing has become an integral element in the way consumers operate day-to-day. And for many new brands, it is the way the customer interacts with the brand.

Yet, while all companies currently reside at different levels of how they integrate digital marketing into their brand efforts, all run the risk of committing the very *faux pas* that may hinder future progress and success. Let's look at the 10 most common digital marketing mistakes that brands and marketers make today, while also offering advice on how companies, and especially marketers, can modify their perspective as they work to realign their mindset with respect to digital marketing and branding:

ONE. Traditional marketing and digital marketing teams frequently operate as two separate entities. Just as entire organizations cannot function properly with siloed departments in place, marketing teams cannot succeed if traditional and digital channels remain divided. Thus, these disparate teams act cautiously, disregarding innovation and advanced strategies as neither group wants to run the risk of losing budget to the more effective channel.

WHAT TO DO: Break down silos to develop an informed cross-channel branding strategy. If companies truly want to run integrated, cross-channel campaigns, they must create an organizational structure that supports that very philosophy. Ultimately, such integrated teams can leverage historical data captured by traditional means over the years to guide digital programs and initiatives, while also leveraging digital to test new approaches and programs before investing in traditional media.

TWO. Companies often attempt to rush progress via digital marketing because they can move faster, inevitably implementing the wrong technology and creating confusion. Many brands lack vision, planning, and commitment when they first enact their digital marketing strategies. Thus, marketers rush to choose a product or technology via marketing that may not be able to solve the important problems at hand. Implementing the incorrect marketing strategy at the start may inevitably warrant another partnership or product to manage in the future, leading teams to underperform.

WHAT TO DO: Establish goals, develop plans, and research available technologies prior to adoption. Before companies can verify the proper technology, they must establish goals and develop plans that will guide their journey forward. However, jumping on the slick new product bandwagon may become costly. Therefore, once KPIs (critical performance indicators) have been determined, marketers must thoroughly research the available marketing platforms and tools in the market to ensure that the solution is the right fit for their needs, will integrate with existing platforms, and can scale with their growing needs.

THREE. Digital marketers implement programs simply because they can. Though counterintuitive, many digital marketers implement programs that lack purpose and diminish trust. For instance, marketers will create loyalty programs despite the fact that they provide no loyalty incentives whatsoever. They look to collect customer data, but they fail to offer any rewards or tailored engagements in return.

WHAT TO DO: Make sure all initiatives drive value and support trust. Poorly planned and unsupported initiatives may drive customers to the competition, as they detract from the ability to truly engage and convert consumers and actually hurt the brand. Thus, digital marketers must refrain from running to the latest tools because focusing on fewer initiatives that deliver value will positively impact trust more than any scattered strategy in the marketplace.

FOUR. Brands produce content for the sake of having content rather than offer relevant messaging that speaks to customers' specific interests. Most brands believe the ability to post and share content across channels means they must produce an endless flood of information. Marketers understand that customer interactions take place across all touchpoints, leading them to believe that they must provide a constant stream of content no matter the platform, for they believe that visibility will result in engagement when, in reality, this strategy typically diminishes interest and again could hurt the brand.

WHAT TO DO: Post engaging content that demonstrates the importance of quality over quantity. Because content has clearly become an integral element of the digital marketing experience, companies must approach this trend carefully, as other brands have also hopped on the bandwagon. Instead of focusing on quantity, marketers must focus on the quality of their content. Engaging material has the power to strengthen customer loyalty and advocacy, while mediocre content will likely have the opposite effect.

FIVE. Marketers think they can (and should) monitor and measure every customer interaction point possible. Though marketers now have the ability to gather, analyze, and act upon data across the customer lifecycle, many will find that the power of digital can also hinder progress. Most marketers find themselves drowning in a sea of unnecessary data because they insist on tracking everything imaginable. Ultimately, however, not all customer information and behavioral data can be brought to action, nor should it be.

WHAT TO DO: Take one step at a time to determine which touchpoints and metrics truly impact the bottom line. Marketers must develop a better balance via constant testing and strategy reconfiguration. Not every touchpoint will yield information that pertains to the brand's bottom line, and these relevant touchpoints are likely to change as the customer experience evolves. Sometimes less is more.

SIX. Marketers dream of a multi-channel strategy, but fail to centralize the incoming digital data. For years, marketers have romanticized the notion of a multi-channel experience. Yet, while many talk about breaking down the departmental silos that stall progress, few have successfully implemented this unified approach to customer experience and data collection, as companies typically lack a cohesive organizational structure, as well as the technological infrastructure to bring all incoming information together under one roof.

WHAT TO DO: Integrate customer information to understand the customer experience and drive strategic development. Ultimately, data centralization will be the primary component standing between success and failure; companies that neglect to integrate disparate systems are destined to struggle, hindering customer experience. When it comes to data centralization, organizations must invest in the integrated technologies that enable marketers to be more efficient and effective with regard to actionable decision-making. Ideally, companies will have such a marketing infrastructure in place from the start, as those who fail to implement such systems are destined to fight an uphill battle against resource decisions, siloed information, and enterprise wide inefficiencies. Unfortunately, however, such is the case for many on the journey toward digital proficiency, as few brands currently have the ability to blend incoming data across the entire organization.

SEVEN. Marketers, especially digital marketers, rarely look to consumer behavior for guidance, ultimately failing to uphold the brand promise. Despite the fact that consumer behavior ultimately drives brand success or failure, many marketers neglect to tap into said actions to derive insight from this incoming data. These companies rush to implement the latest digital strategy because it's the newest trend. But seeking solutions from this "business first" standpoint signals the wrong approach, as marketers disregard their own customers' needs, desires, bad experiences, and demands for brand engagement.

WHAT TO DO: Put the customer in the center of your marketing strategy to boost trust and deliver ROI (return on investment). By organizing campaigns that build upon customer insight, brands can easily strengthen trust in order to cultivate the types of relationships necessary for continued success. Ultimately, digital campaigns can't succeed based on Big Data and analytics alone. Instead, marketers must consider clear and actionable customer insights. Delivering the perfectly tailored message to the intended target remains at the core of every marketer's mission. However, digital marketing will always be secondary to an actual relationship; this is why companies must maintain a real, humanistic approach to their marketing and branding efforts.

EIGHT. Executives invest in the necessary marketing technology, but not the resources that drive success. While most leaders now agree that digital channels require special attention, many invest time and money into integrating the proper systems, yet few invest in the necessary resources. Companies often thrust management responsibilities on their already tapped-out workforces, setting the initiative up for failure from the onset.

WHAT TO DO: Create teams that specifically care for and carry out the brand's digital strategy. Technology isn't going to operate itself. Instead, strategic development must also include finding the right person or team of people with the necessary skillset and bandwidth to make the investment worthwhile. Ultimately, brands must recognize that technology cannot replace employees, for the customer experience will always require the human touch.

NINE. Brands neglect to establish one brand manager to monitor metrics and goals. Because companies often implement marketing initiatives with great speed, many use this "bias for action" as an excuse for not taking the time to develop comprehensive plans and well-defined campaigns with specific objectives. Thus, employees begin operating within their siloed departments without one brand manager to oversee and manage the results of the marketing campaigns. What is the goal: brand awareness, leads or sales?

WHAT TO DO: Understand how each digital asset performs and its contribution to the end goal. By putting one brand manager in the position to supervise all marketing activity, companies will ultimately come to understand the role of each digital asset with regard to how they individually and collectively impact the broader campaign. Thus, brands can easily create one comprehensive snapshot of the campaign and demonstrate how each asset contributes to the end goal so the brand manager may effectively shift budget dollars to maximize marketing campaign performance.

TEN. Marketing teams lack the company-wide buy-in needed to advance digital strategy development. As with every company initiative, digital marketing requires top-down buy-in if said strategies hope to succeed. Implementation isn't something that can be turned on or off by flipping the switch. Marketers need continued support so they may take slow, but steady steps toward success.

WHAT TO DO: Gain executive buy-in and build partner relationships to enable a unified marketing strategy. True commitment must be supported from the top, or else investments in technology, partnerships, infrastructure, and resources will likely lack the fortitude to sustain long-term success. Thus, marketers must establish a clear set of strategic goals and develop a plan with launch milestones and success measurements to ensure all levels of the company are in the loop regarding progress. Developing partnerships with best-in-class providers will also enable marketers to integrate solutions for scalability and expansion. With said relationships in place, companies will be well on their way to establishing a unified marketing strategy that values and benefits the entire organization.

In the end, the customer experience must be at the heart of every digital marketing initiative, for customers will inevitably feel the impact of both failed and successful strategies. It's not about the latest digital marketing technology. It's about the customer and how they feel about the brand. Marketers must proceed with caution, as the customer relationship remains delicate, particularly in this connected age, when the competition is only one click away.

MOVE FIRST OR FOLLOW FAST?

As a marketer, you need to understand the brand challenge of either launching a product or service, taking market share or disrupting a marketplace. Why? Because there are so many unknowns. Are you early to the marketplace? Are you late? Where is the marketplace going? Who will be my future competitor? When we did the branding and marketing for Amazon, there were other booksellers already online. Who were they? Who knows or cares now. We reasoned that we were slightly early to the ecommerce marketplace so we decided to create a powerful brand and position Amazon as a leader. Next, we talked to potential customers, created differentiation via having access to a million book titles, allowed customers to post reviews, one-click remembering you and so on.

MOVE FIRST OR FOLLOW FAST

THE CHALLENGE OF BRANDING TODAY.

We also had the right amount of marketing dollars and founder support to not only create awareness but to build the brand position: *Amazon.com: Earth's Biggest Bookstore.* That in turn drove sales. Lots of sales.

It's awesome if you are the first to move into a market and can take a dominate position. But the competition is always lurking so you better move fast and build defensive brand positions (i.e. unique formula, critical partnership, patents, etc.). And it's still no guarantee that being first will win out. In fact, this is rarely true. Over time, 47% of first-movers fail, compared with only 8% of fast followers. As the phrase goes, you can recognize a marketplace pioneer from the arrows in the companies back.

First-mover advantage isn't automatically bestowed unto the first product in a category. It's not even guaranteed to exist in your industry and, when it does, it is fought for and earned. *It's first winner, not first-mover.* Being first to the market means precisely nothing. Being the first to enter a market brings opportunities which, when exploited, can turn into advantages. First-mover advantages have a shelf-life and must be replaced with long-term differentiators. And you better demonstrate those differences in a way which means something to your customers and empowers your brand. The tactic here is to refine the user experience of the product or service such that it appeals to more than just early adopters. You need to move into early mass customers and then the mass market to succeed. This is what Apple did when they watched Saehan, Diamond Rio, HanGo, Creative Nomad, Cowon, and Archos all launch increasingly more advanced MP3 players to a slow-to-adopt customer. Rather than getting caught in this mess, Apple waited until the technology was sufficiently advanced and the market was sufficiently matured before launching a product with the best brand experience. iPod.

So, if being the first to enter a market is not absolutely critical (think Uber then Lyft), what is then? Some of you might have already guessed. More important than entering the market first is to enter the market *before* someone becomes a dominant brand and then better understand the customer needs, innovate and evolve your product or service to become the dominant brand in the industry. Contrary to what most people think,

King Gillette was not the first to market safety razors. They were invented in 1880 by the Kampfe brothers, and a decade before King Gillette opened his company there were already commercial safety razors being sold. Gillette, however, evolved the product rapidly both by improving the design and by creating a business model where the profits would be made with the disposable blades. Neatly crafted business strategy, good understanding of customer needs and great marketing enabled Gillette to dominate the safety razor market for such a long period of time. And they were not the first to enter the market. Now, they have to deal with a brand disruptor, Dollar Shave Club.

Another challenge you have as marketers has nothing to do with existing companies. It has to do with large customer groups who are changing their needs.

BRANDS, BOOMERS AND MILLENNIALS

While I will go into more depth with these two large customer groups in Chapter Ten, I will briefly review the challenges of branding to baby boomers (aged 56-85) and millennials (aged 18 - 35). Just in the USA, boomers number about 71 million and declining (you could say dying) and about 76 million millennials (81 million by 2025). Currently, there are about two billion millennials worldwide. These two customer segments are incredibly important to marketers. Why? It's not just the sheer numbers. It's the amount of current wealth the boomers have and the amazing wealth the millennials will inherit. So, you better understand what's important to each segment from a branding perspective. Here are some things to keep in mind when targeting either of these two groups with your marketing and branding:

Baby Boomers. They hold massive amounts of wealth, they are living longer, they are more active, they don't want to move into retirement homes and they are actually using technology albeit as late adopters.

Millennials. They love technology, they don't have enough money (or maybe even desire) to buy a house in suburbia, they live in downtown or in lifestyle areas, love to travel, socialize via social media and will care more about social issues and the environment.

If you don't know enough about them or don't have key insights to these two groups, you better read and learn more about them, especially on a global level. Keep your eye on these two groups as they will make and break brands. Better yet, understand the benefits you need to build into your brand in order to be successful.

BRAND INSIGHT

This $11 billion entertainment industry could not get out of its own way when renegade companies and customers start to decimate its sales by getting its products through other channels, albeit illegally. Industry leaders and executives of major brands argued for over three years about how to solve the problem. One person seemed to understand the problem and his company had the brand permission from its customer base to launch a new sub-brand called iTunes. iTunes created the first legal music store online, made buying music online fashionable with its silhouette campaign, leveled the playing field for independent artists and labels, created the simple "single" price and helped to slow the erosion of all out piracy. You can argue the long-term effect of "singles" pricing but it definitely jump-started the legal sale of music online. And it did not hurt iPod sales either. Regardless of how it turns out now that we have streaming music, Apple leveraged its brand equity and really made the first powerful step of becoming a consumer goods company and not just a computer company. They evolved their brand before the competition forced their hand.

KEY TAKEAWAY

Your brand needs to evolve to stay relevant as your customers change. If you build a powerful brand that customers love, they will give you permission to introduce a new product or service that *they* believe you have the capability and the where with all to fulfill their needs. That is what we call an amazing brand.

CHAPTER FOUR
THE BENEFITS OF BRANDING.
* * *

The world is full of products. Amazon **alone** sells over 500 million products through its website. Most of these products are a commodity. While that is not necessarily bad, it means there is a substitute product for every product sold. While that may be perfectly fine for someone selling on price, it does not work for creating a powerful brand where "emotion" can be more powerful than financial value or even another similar product. Let me explain. Products perform a function. They have properties that when combined together do something for customers. The problem is that within any given category, most products perform similar functions. There's very little differentiation. Ingredients are ingredients and they tend to be the same across a category. Products are all about what they do for people. Products fulfill a customer's needs. Functions, ingredients and needs — that's what makes up a product.

Brands are different. Brands offer an emotion. Brands are actually quite different from products because they don't just cover a customer's *needs*, they fulfill a customer's *wants*. We don't fall in love with products — we fall in love with brands. Brands offer a promise and an emotion. Brands are about how they make people feel. Promises, emotions and wants — that's what makes up a brand. It's a big difference. In short, while you may need a product, you will want a brand you can trust.

So for example, I may need a cup of tea, but I personally want to get it at Starbucks. Tea is the product in this case and caffeine is the ingredient. I need it to get going in the morning and I could get it literally anywhere, including at Dunkin' Donuts, the corner market or at home. But I choose Starbucks. Starbucks is the brand in this case, and the experience at Starbucks is the emotion I want in the morning. I want a Starbucks tea because of the unique experience I get and how it makes me feel. It prepares me for the day ahead and makes me productive in the morning. With Starbucks tea, I am ready! I want Starbucks for how it makes me feel. Products equal functions. Brands equal emotions. Hopefully you can see that products are basically at parity to each other, they fulfill the same needs. Brands are what differentiate the products because of how they uniquely make people feel. What happens when, as a marketer, you focus on product marketing versus branding?

PRODUCTS JUST CAN'T SURVIVE OVER TIME

Early in my career, without really understanding branding, I created amazing product marketing campaigns that did well and led to product sales. But it was a vicious cycle. Do more marketing to sell more products. Sell more products, do more marketing. Eventually we were always competing on price as we were selling commodities. And if a good brand was falling out of favor with its current customers and they did not change to meet customer needs and wants, then one of two things always happened. One, they lost market share and the company response was to do promotions effectively lowering price and devaluing the product and the brand. The second, and worse scenario, was the company ignored the problem and went into a freefall eventually heading for bankruptcy or sale to a competitor. Think Borders or Blockbuster.

I am watching one such scenario right now with a product you know. GoPro. GoPro was launched in 2002 so it's more than 15 years old. When they launched, they offered the world an amazingly small camera that was seen as new and innovative even though it was really just a new form factor. It had most of the ingredients, along with a waterproof case, of any small camera. I assumed over time that they would evolve to become a powerful brand that understood that they were not selling cameras but were helping customer's create memories. So I kept waiting for the "brand" to evolve into new products, maybe an online easy to use editing portal that would distribute all the "memories" into people's social media dynamically. Or better yet, evolve into a line of consumer products like wireless remote cameras, the new RING replacement for doorbells, security, etc. Well, that did not happen. GoPro grew on back of the rising popularity of social media not on its unique value. Guess what? Smartphones came along and had improved cameras. And it seems that everyone who wanted a GoPro has bought one. Now the competitors are arriving from offshore and prices are falling. GoPro's stock price has fallen from $87 to $9 dollars a share. Ouch. I don't necessarily want any company to fail. The marketplace and customers will decide that. But I do know one thing. GoPro never built a brand and now they are paying the price for being a commodity product.

UNDERSTAND THE DIFFERENCE BETWEEN BRANDING AND MARKETING

Product marketing vs. brand marketing: Separate your product or seperate your customers? Product marketing differentiates your products from other products. Brand marketing differentiates your customers from other customers.

Imagine walking on a solid, enormous, continuous surface presenting all the possible features of products in a category. Customers can and do wander anywhere along the surface. Over here is higher quality, walk over there and the price goes down, walk over here and the product gets faster and more efficient. Product marketing inherently assumes this continuous surface connects all the products customers can consider as competitors. Think of this surface as the marketplace. Product marketers look for differentiation. They look for a spot on this surface they can own. And when things go exactly right, they look for customers to self-select based on a deep preference for that spot in the landscape.

In this sense, the Holy Grail for both brand and product marketing is differentiation. But how differentiation is defined in each case is very different.

Differentiation in product marketing is the perceived separation between your product and your competition on this continuous feature surface. The ideal positioning is a spot only you occupy and therefore what you offer is defensible. Often these spots are different in ways only you recognize as significant. This is a mindset known as the "narcissism of small differences" to anthropologists. In feudal times, you can imagine a feudal lord finding this position and building a fort to defend it so no one else can occupy that spit of land. However, if you are small it is likely your fort is trivial and weak. And it is likely that one of the bigger land owners will be able to overwhelm the territory if they try.

Brand marketing is different. With brand marketing you're attempting to create an island disconnected from this surface. Brand marketing is realizing that your goal is to separate your customers, not your product. You are creating your own island. A discontinuous piece of land that may be hard to reach, but it is just as hard to leave. You are creating separation in the customers' decision process for your product versus your competitors', not on features, but personal identity. You are trying to get your customers to see themselves as the kind of people that look for options all over your island, and not over on that other larger surface of land where you would likely be almost defenseless against competitive onslaught.

If your customers feel like they have voluntarily left that continuous surface of features to be with their own kind and travel to your island, they will find themselves traveling on only that feature surface. They will ask which iPad version to buy or which dog breed or which Levi's shirt. But their consideration of options won't leave the island. After all, they are BMW people, not Cadillac people. Dog people, not cat people.

For a competitor to get those customers to leave your island to go to the other surface of land, to earn consideration, is wildly more difficult than anything we have discussed so far. They need to make the person willing to get up and swim, give up where they have been and change their identity. The force this takes, what chemists call the "activation energy," is dramatically higher. If life on the island gets really bad, folks will flee, but they don't do it lightly. Rationale? Of course, the dog person says dogs are

THE BENEFITS OF BRANDING. 54

friendlier. The Levi's person justifies a higher price based on quality. The BMW owner says Cadillac makes boring cars. But the truth is not in these descriptions. The truth is, these people simply do not consider anything in the other category when they're trying to figure out how to meet their desires and needs. They are BMW people, dog people, and Levi's people. And they honestly believe there is no substitute for their brands. So how do you differentiate your brand?

THE BRAND IS THE DIFFERENCE

So, now that you are beginning to understand just how critical it is to focus on branding, and more importantly, to differentiate your brand, how do you go about it? This is a critical phase because you can usually only launch a brand or company once. When we launched the Amazon branding, we focused on being different with the breadth of book titles (over 1 million), amazing customer engagement (remembering who you were, allowing you to write reviews, etc.) and a positioning out of the gate that was to establish Amazon as a leader in the book selling category: *Earth's Biggest Bookstore.*

Here are some insights on how you could potentially differentiate a brand:

PRICE DIFFERENTLY. You can be either the economy bestseller with a low price, or a premium brand with a high price – such as Starbucks, which prices coffee higher to increase perceived quality. In fact, many brand differentiation strategies can help you charge and receive a premium price.

OWN A NICHE AND THEN EXPAND. Niche products or services have built-in brand differentiation, and the marketing for them should reflect that niche. A good example is Nike which started out just making running shoes. Once they owned that category, they expanded.

BE THE EXPERT. If your brand is the best at something in your industry, you can differentiate by focusing on your expertise. Domino's Pizza provides differentiation through its expert home delivery and 30-minute guarantee.

USE A MASCOT OR SPOKESPERSON. Brand mascots can be powerful differentiators, especially if you want to bring a sense of humor to your brand perceptions. GEICO has created massive success with its mascot – a talking lizard that has nothing to do with insurance, but still makes millions of people believe there's something different about the company. Be careful, though, as this could backfire as it did with Subway.

INNOVATE. Innovation can be a key brand differentiator. This type of distinctiveness is common for tech brands – Apple is synonymous with innovation, ease of use and enhanced life experiences. SalesForce captured a large market share with a cloud-based CRM. Uber does not have any cars but united millions of drivers to pick you up.

BE THE UNDERDOG. A lot of customers love a good underdog story and will connect with you through your 'David and Goliath' brand story. Emphasizing your brand's humble beginnings can help you differentiate, especially if your competitors are focused on being the biggest and the best. Sir Richard Branson has launched the Virgin brand into multiple sectors with a 'David and Goliath' strategy, challenging the perceived big guys and the status quo as the "customer's champion."

CONSISTENTLY OVER-DELIVER ON CUSTOMER SERVICE. With all other factors equal to your competitors, consistently superior customer service and exceeding expectations can differentiate your brand. Online shoe store Zappos commands a premium price tier because of their outstanding customer service, including free shipping and free returns. They don't even make shoes.

TELL YOUR UNIQUE BRAND STORY. Every successful brand has a compelling story behind it. Fully developing and emphasizing your brand story can help you differentiate, be core to your brand DNA, and reinforce the personality, promise and values of your brand. Volcom, the action sports brand started with a story supported with a *"youth against establishment"* marketing position.

APPEAL TO EMOTIONS. Your brand can stand out by delivering an emotional experience that's associated with your product or service. Coca-Cola capitalizes on emotional appeal by branding their products as happy, implying it's the maker of joy and harmony. Everything Coca-Cola does from a strategic branding perspective is to associate the brand with "happy occasions." Too bad more people are drinking juice and water. ☺ Oh, is that why Coco-Cola is buying water and juice brands.

PERSONIFY YOUR PRODUCT. A slightly different strategy from brand mascots, brand personification involves creating a "character" that represents the characteristics of your brand. Green Giant, which sells vegetables, has done this successfully with the Jolly Green Giant, while Keebler snacks are personified through the Keebler Elves.

GIVE BACK. Modern customers, most notably Millennials, love to get behind a brand that gives back to the community. By emphasizing corporate social responsibility (CSR), you can differentiate your brand and get an edge over the competition such as Tom's shoe company.

REDEFINE YOUR PRODUCT USE. If your products can accomplish more than one thing, the alternate use can help you differentiate your brand. As an example, Arm & Hammer was just another baking soda until the brand began marketing the idea that it also made an excellent air freshener along with a multitude of other uses.

PROVIDE HIGHER QUALITY. Luxury brands are able to command premium pricing through an emphasis on higher quality products – either actual or perceived. Providing luxury is an automatic brand differentiator for most markets as it has done for Coach, Rolex, Porsche and a host of other luxury brands.

CREATE A NEW CATEGORY. When a marketplace gets very large and is still growing, consider creating a new sub-category within the larger marketplace. This is exactly what Vitamin Water did (in the bottled water marketplace) and it benefited tremendously with its focus on its association with vitamins.

No matter the strategy you use, you have to create brand differentiation in your customer's minds and have them "feel" there is no good substitute for your product or service. And the benefits of good brand differentiation are very important.

THE BENEFITS OF GREAT BRANDING

The benefits of great branding are critically important to a company. It will hopefully yield better pricing, better gross margin, higher level of consideration, higher degree of trust, respect from your customers and most importantly, customer empathy. This is what allows Starbucks to sell a cup of coffee that costs them about $1.20 for about $4.

Branding provides the entire company with several key benefits:

BRANDING PROVIDES A COMPETITIVE ADVANTAGE. Whether you're a non-profit or a for-profit, your organization needs to compete for resources, funding and talent, and audience attention. To win your category, organizations plan and implement strategy and create a roadmap that outlines specific actions and measures for reaching their goals and out maneuvering their peers for needed resources. When done correctly the organization's brand mirrors their strategic plan, and helps promote strategic areas and initiatives that will move the organization forward.

BRANDS PROVIDE A STABLE ASSET. Products might fail, companies are bought and sold, technologies change on a daily basis, but strong brands carry on through all these changes. Brands are the most sustainable asset of any organization, and when aligned with the overall strategy of the organization they can function as the central organizing principle for the organization's decision making. Consider that the Coca-Cola brand has been around for more than 120 years, while most of the world's other valued brands have existed for just 50 years, and most corporations only last 25 years.

BRANDS PROVIDE ECONOMIC VALUE. The value of organizations is divided into two areas: intangible and tangible assets—brands being intangible assets. A study of organizations in the S&P 500 index showed that over a 30-year period between 1975 and 2003 the overall corporate value of intangible assets increased from 17% to 80%. The business magazine, Businessweek, has concluded that brands account for more than one-third of shareholder value. This leaves us with the conclusion that the value of most businesses comes from intangible assets, brands being the most prominent of these assets. Consider that the Coca-Cola brand name alone is worth $79 billion and accounts for over 54% of the stock market value of the organization. Because of their financial impact, brands are a unique organizational asset. Brands play a key role in attracting employees, partners and most importantly audiences to an organization. Brands help cut through the clutter of the marketplace, creating awareness for organizations and helping them attract and develop the mutually beneficial relationships with customers, suppliers and the public that they need to reach their goals.

BRANDS SET EXPECTATIONS. We live in a world based on promises. The airline mechanic promises to do a thorough job, checking and rechecking the aircraft to make sure it's safe. Restaurants promise to provide fresh food made in clean environments. Our teachers promise to educate and protect our children during the school day. At the heart of branding is the promise that is made by the organization to their customers. The brand promise tells the customers who you are, what you believe in, and what unique value you provide. The ability to fulfill your promises at every stage of the relationship is the defining factor for most organizations' success or failure. When promises are broken the reputation of the organization is called into question and the brand suffers. When brand promises are kept, audiences respond with loyalty and affection.

THE POWER OF EMOTIONAL BRAND BENEFITS

Many marketers would agree that we buy some products and services that enhance our positive sense of self-esteem in some way. We believe that all brands, products and their features are associated with a rewarding emotional payoff. Moreover, all features and benefits are linked to emotional end benefits. Think of brands like Apple, Samsung, Fiji Water, Mercedes, Ford, Starbucks, Dunkin' Donuts, Hershey, Godiva, Tiffany, Nike, Coach, and Disneyland. We seek out these brands with their USPs (unique selling proposition), features and functional benefits because we like the way they make us feel and what they allow us to communicate about ourselves. But let's backtrack for a moment. People get confused between emotions and emotional benefits. There is an important distinction between them that marketers need to understand.

An "emotion" is best defined as a state of physiological arousal to which we attach a cognitive label. Let's assume there are only four core emotions" mad, glad, scared and sad. Knowing how our brand, features and functions or brand activity (concepts, advertising, names, taglines, etc.) makes someone "feel" is only minimallyuseful. We definitely want to know if our marketing makes people feel "glad" or

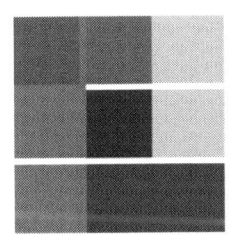

EMOTIONAL VS. RATIONAL BENEFITS

"bad, "but that is ONLY a measure of valence; it does little or nothing to lend direction to our creative efforts. It tells us nothing about how to set the mood and tone for our advertising or even necessarily how to FIX any bad feelings that emerge. It is the "emotional benefit" and not the raw "emotion" that is most informative, motivating and useful for brand development. An emotional benefit, not a physiological state of arousal with a simplistic label, is an often complex, positive, cognitive statement that our respondents are able to make about themselves due to their use, display and attachment to our brand and its features.

More succinctly, an emotional benefit is nothing more than "something nice" I can say about myself because I use your product or service. Now, armed with this more precise definition of an emotional benefit, let me proceed to discuss exactly how emotional benefits influence purchase and branding. Emotional benefits, although mostly unconscious, are attached to specific elements of a brand and to the brand itself as a whole. You can actually think of them entirely without reference to the word "emotion" and remain fully in the rational sphere, if you prefer, because it is really just the "kind of person" that a particular rational feature supports. The emotional benefit or value is the adjectivo describing the self. See the examples below and it will make sense:

> I am an attractive person because I chose this particular long-lasting lipstick.

I am a productive person because I purchased an iPhone with a fast microprocessor.

I am a sexy person because I drive an aerodynamic car.

I am a powerful person because I bought a rowing machine from an infomercial with that muscular guy.

I am an energetic person because I replenish electrolytes after exercise with Gatorade.

In other words, your brand needs to create that emotional benefit in the customers mind because EVERY rational feature is desired for the support of some aspect of self-concept. EVERY LAST ONE! Emotional benefits are able to wield their influence precisely because they work behind the scenes, beyond the awareness of the customer. It is the very fact that they are so elusive and hidden that makes them so very powerful and persuasive. In other words, you can't say what you want the customer to feel. For example, If you were to read the above benefit statements (e.g., "I am a sexy person because I drive an aerodynamic car") to a customer directly and ask for levels of agreement, you would get a much lower level of agreement than is, in fact, the case, and market behavior would differ greatly from what you tried to evaluate in your research. Why? Because emotional motivation usually operates below the surface, beyond the ability of respondents to easily access and articulate. People do not want to believe that they are emotionally influenced towards brands or purchase. They find the idea repugnant and aversive. The fact that people do not want to admit to using brands as a method of partially supporting their self-esteem forces these associations out of consciousness, and it prevents people from cognitively reasoning about emotional benefits or articulating them out loud. In fact, many brands make the mistake of raising the emotional benefits to a level of awareness that takes away their power. They try to FORCE the psychological insight benefit by telling the consumer directly. This doesn't work nearly as well as INDIRECTLY communicating these benefits via an emphasis on specifying the features and functions of the brand that support them, while the creative mood and tone of marketing communications convey the emotional benefit. The ultimate end emotional benefit or value is always enhanced by the self-esteem of the customer.

So, as a marketer, if you want your brand to create a "feeling" inside the customers' mind, you need to understand how your product or service creates a sense of positive self-worth to your target customer. Then, via branding and marketing messaging, you can create that feeling inside them and have them say, "I love my iPhone."

BRAND INSIGHT

This company got its start through a single founder in the 1960's. He started the company quite by accident when he fashioned some unique climbing gear to help him and his friends climb more safely. Over the years, the company started to grow and they added other products that were not only different in color and style but they were designed better. By no means did the company have a smooth ride in its growth. Sales went up, sales went down. At some point, sales really began to grow consistently and the founders asked themselves, "What do we want to be known for as a company? How do we want our customers to feel about us? What brand are we creating?" That led to deep introspection and out of that came a core set of values and a mission. Build the best product, cause no unnecessary harm, use business to inspire and implement solutions to the environmental crisis. Patagonia was on its way to becoming a powerful brand that creates not just climbing gear and clothes. It creates a feeling in their customers' minds that there is no substitute for not buying the best outdoor clothing from a brand that is helping the planet. I love my Patagonia vest.

KEY TAKEAWAY

Brands can be built very purposefully. It's not about marketing. It's about having a set of values and a mission and then building a brand that communicates those values in such a way that it creates a unique emotional benefit within your customers' hearts and minds.

CHAPTER FIVE
THE STRATEGY BEHIND THE BRAND.
* * *

In 1995, I got a phone call from my partner and CEO of our marketing agency. I was in Portland, Oregon at the time and he was in our corporate office in Cupertino, California in a building we had purchased from Apple. We had gone public earlier that year and our integrated marketing agency was on an insane growth trajectory. We were basically tripling in size each year. So, we were all very busy. Our Portland office was working on putting a local beer brand, Widmer, into bottles nationally, doing solid marketing work for Mitsubishi Motors, consulting on digital strategies with Nike, and although we did not know it, we were only 2-3 months out from winning the Amazon account.

After some casual talk between us, he indicated the reason for his call. He had received a phone call from a well-known venture capitalist at Sequoia Capital. That VC indicated they had just made a $3 million dollar investment in what essentially were two college kids and what they hoped would be a powerful Internet based company. My partner indicated that all three offices in California were crazy busy, they had no bandwidth, and with our early work in digital branding and marketing, could we take on the company as a new client. I asked what the account basically needed. He said they needed branding, design and marketing help. I asked him, "What is the company's brand or marketing strategy?" He said, "I have no clue." I asked, "Well, what is their business model?" He said, "I have no clue." So, as a partner, I leaned in and indicated we would take on Yahoo! as our new client. We worked with them for several months. It was crazy. We eventually designed their logo, redesigned their website and added several other valuable elements. But we could never get the founders or the new company executives to settle on ANY strategy. They simply never could get the team to agree on almost anything. That core problem led them years later to bypass the acquisition of Google. They simply could not agree on a price even though it probably would have propelled them to another level. Or perhaps they would have messed that up. Who knows? Funny thing is, Yahoo! still does not have a brand strategy today. Or a sustainable business model. The company was recently sold to Verizon and who knows what they are going to do with it.

What's the moral of the Yahoo! story? If you are creating a brand or are working in a brand today, you better have several key elements figured out before you do your marketing. Like what is your mission, what are your values, what is your brand strategy, who is your target customer, what's happening with the competition, what's your business model and what kind of marketing campaign will be effective in meeting your strategic company goals. I know that's a lot of thinking going on in one sentence. But I cannot tell you how many brands I have worked with in my career that did not have the above figured out and it led to complete chaos. This would ultimately lead to bad brand and marketing work with these dysfunctional clients. Honestly, by 1996, our marketing agency had become so well recognized, had received top awards and a high "C" level of awareness (recognition from CEO's, COO's, CFO's, etc.) we started turning down opportunities to work with, who we perceived, were unorganized or disruptive clients. Out of every potential client I talked to between 1996 and 1998, I turned 8 out of 10 down. I simply told them we were too busy. The real reason was they were going to be so dysfunctional, it would have negatively impacted the morale and value of our employees, and ultimately, our brand. Learning to say "no" can be a good thing. Especially if a company or brand does not have their act together. Not to be harsh but sometimes you "can't fix stupid."

So before you can actually figure out how to develop a strategy for a brand, you need to know what makes up a brand.

THE CORE ELEMENTS OF A BRAND

The concept of branding can be a confusing topic that many seasoned marketers don't clearly understand let alone the new digital marketers. What is a brand? What is branding? It seems like a simple question, but the answer is anything but simple. If you're confused by your brand, your customers will be confused, too. The last thing you want to do is waste time and money by developing a weak brand. With all the definitions of branding out there, I am going to focus it down to just five components.

THE BRAND PROMISE. At its core, a brand is a promise to consumers. What will consumers get when they purchase a product or service under your brand umbrella? The brand promise incorporates more than just those tangible products and services. It also includes the feelings that consumers get when they use your products and services. Example: Think about your favorite brand and what that brand promises to you. If you're a Nike fan, the brand might represent athleticism, performance, strength, good health, and fun. Your brand promises something to consumers. What is it?

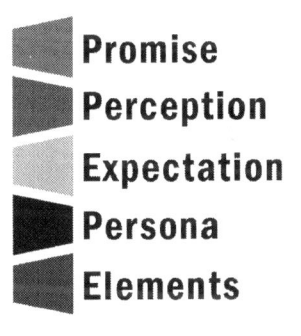

Promise
Perception
Expectation
Persona
Elements

CORE BRAND ATTRIBUTES

THE BRAND PERCEPTIONS. Brands are built by consumers, not companies. Ultimately, it's the way consumers perceive a brand that defines it. It doesn't matter what you think your brand promises. The only thing that matters is how consumers perceive your brand. You need to work to develop consumer perceptions that accurately reflect your brand or else your brand is doomed to limited growth potential. Example: What are consumers' perceptions of Lady Gaga? You can bet everything she does is meant to create specific consumer perceptions.

THE BRAND EXPECTATIONS. **Based on your brand promise, consumers develop expectations for your brand.** When they pull their hard-earned money out of their pockets and purchase your products or services, they assume their expectations for your brand will be met. If your brand doesn't meet consumers expectations in every interaction, consumers will become confused by your brand and turn away from it in search of another brand that does meet their expectations in every interaction. Example: Imagine if Porsche launched a $10,000 car. To say the least, consumers would be extremely confused because such a product doesn't meet their expectations for a luxury performance brand.

THE BRAND PERSONA. Rather than asking, "What is a brand?" a better question might be, "Who is a brand?" Every brand has a persona. Think of your brand as a person. What is that person like? What can you expect when you interact with that person? From appearance to personality and everything in between, your brand persona is one that consumers will evaluate and judge before they do business with you. Example: Think of it this way. Who would you rather spend time with if they were a person, Apple or Microsoft? These two brands have very different brand personas. Your brand should have one, too.

THE BRAND ELEMENTS. Your brand is represented by the intangible elements described above as well as tangible elements such as your brand logo, messaging, packaging, marketing and so on. All of these elements must work together in an integrated way to consistently communicate your brand promise, shape brand perceptions, meet brand expectations, and define your brand persona. If one element is awry, your entire brand can suffer. Remember what happened with the new Gap logo introduced a few years ago? Customers hated it. Don't make the same mistake. Example: There is a reason why that blue Tiffany's box has been around for so long. It means something to consumers.

Bottom-line, a brand is clear, reliable, and believable to both your consumers and your employees. However, brands aren't built overnight. Before you can define and live your brand, you need to do some research so you don't waste time taking your brand in a direction that won't allow you to reach your goals. You must understand your competitors and target audience so that you can develop a brand that promises the right things to the right people. Research should be first, definition, strategy, and marketing implementation should follow, and in time, your brand will grow.

AIM YOUR BRAND FOR A BLUE OCEAN

In an earlier chapter I talked about a form of research called Observation Lab that you can use to get customer insights by observing them in their environment. But if you want a more strategic view, say from 10,000 feet, of an entire marketplace, including the competition, then you need to elevate your perspective and examine an entire market. One methodology you could use would be Blue Ocean Strategy. I love using blue ocean strategy in the classroom. I loved using it in my professional life. It's so simple to understand and it forces the students, and perhaps marketers, to answer really simple questions regarding a current product or service:

- What can I eliminate?
- What can I reduce?
- What can I raise the bar on?
- What can I create that is new?

BLUE OCEAN STRATEGY

You can set sail for a blue ocean all in the hopes of creating a new product or service in a growing marketplace with little initial competition. Blue Ocean Strategy by Chan Kim and Renee Mauborgne was published in 2005 by Harvard Business School Press. It became a best-seller and still remains popular today. The authors' thesis is that most companies focus on competing against rivals for market share in existing marketplaces. I will provide you with more insights and some detailed information on how to use Blue Ocean strategy in Chapter Ten.

WHY DO BLUE OCEANS MATTER?

Blue oceans matter because these markets are potentially large and with less competition, so there is more opportunity for you to grow as the dominant brand as long as you continue to innovate. Let's look at a real example of a company that created a blue ocean all for themselves. Cirque du Soleil, the Canadian company, redefined the dynamics of a declining circus industry in the 1980s. Under conventional strategic business analysis, the circus industry was a loser. Star performers had "supplier power" over the company. Alternative forms of entertainment, from sporting events to home entertainment systems, were relatively inexpensive and on the rise. Moreover, animal rights groups were putting increased pressure on circuses for their treatment of animals. Cirque du Soleil eliminated the animals and reduced the importance of individual stars. It created a new form of entertainment that combined dance, music, and athletic skill to appeal to an upscale adult audience that had abandoned the traditional circus. Cirque du Soleil attracted a new customer, mostly adults as opposed to children, at a high price point, and redefined what a circus is supposed to be. Today, Cirque du Soleil has a valuation of over $2.5 billion.

Let's examine another tool you can use to define a "brand opportunity space" in an existing marketplace.

CREATING A PERCEPTION MAP FOR YOUR BRAND

Perceptual maps are an important element in determining marketing strategy for your brand. First, what are perceptual maps? *"Perceptual mapping is a graphics technique used by marketers that attempts to visually display the perceptions of customers or potential customers. Typically the position of a product, product line, brand, or company is displayed relative to their competition."* Although perceptual maps (also called product positioning maps) can have any number of dimensions thanks to the wonders of modern computers, commonly perceptual maps are graphed on two dimensions for clarity and simplicity. Why would you want to do perceptual mapping? Perceptual maps help you understand what consumers think about your brand and your competitor's brand. Most importantly, perceptual maps help you build an effective marketing strategy by visually identifying potential gaps or areas of a marketplace that are possible opportunities to exploit.

I think it might help you see how valuable perceptual maps are by showing you an example. Know that you can chart any industry or marketplace and determine where you brand might be today and where it might have to be tomorrow. This kind of mapping also identifies potential "gaps" in the marketplace that might actually be potential blue oceans for your brand. I started my marketing career in Detroit and worked with every major automotive brand there and then with Mercedes Benz in New Jersey. So, as an example, let's look at the automotive industry. This example maps automobile companies based on two criteria; sporty versus conservative and practical/affordable versus classy/distinctive. The key element in perceptual mapping, from the standpoint of marketing strategy, is the axis should measure attitudes related to something that determines which products/brands consumers purchase.

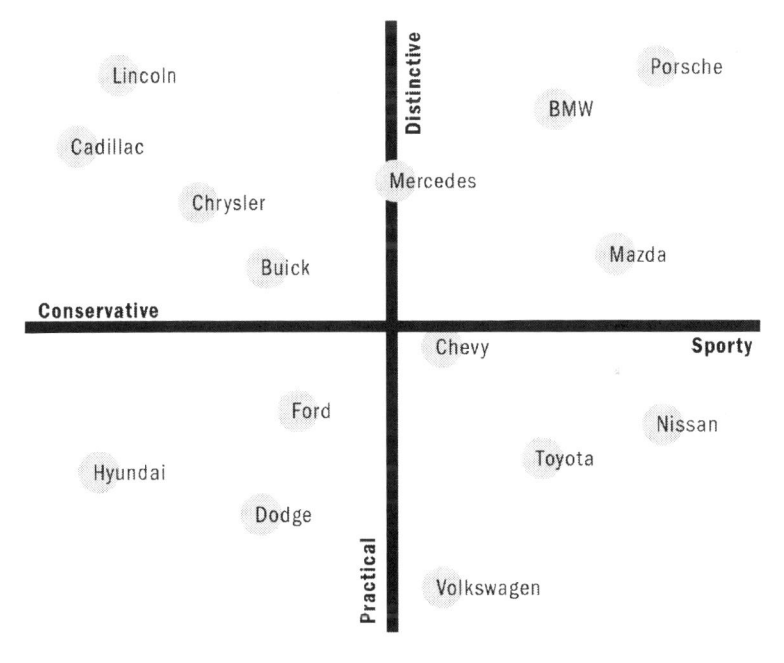

MARKETPLACE PERCEPTION MAP

From the standpoint of marketing strategy, the key element in perceptual mapping lies in the axis; it should measure attitudes related to something that determines which products/brands consumers purchase.

THE STRATEGY BEHIND THE BRAND.

If you look at the perception map, you will see where I have placed these brands based on where customers perceive them to be based on research. Creating perceptual maps will give you a sense of where your brand stands among all the completive brands in your marketplace. If you agree, awesome. If you don't agree, your brand is in potential trouble. Also, if you look at the map, you can see some potential "opportunity" gaps. Look in the lower right quadrant. There seems to be an opportunity to create a brand that is sporty and affordable. In the lower left quadrant, perhaps you could create a brand that is conservative and affordable. If that's what customers want or better yet, need. And that is the critical point of view you need to have when creating perceptual maps. It's has to be based on what customers believe today and potentially want tomorrow. Not what you want or what you believe.

Now that we understand what a perceptual map is and why we should create one for any brand, let's talk about how you construct one.

1. Determine which characteristics of the product are consumer hot buttons. This is going to be a function of your market, so the characteristics that consumers use to determine which car to buy are entirely different from which doctor to use, where the criterion might be reputation (high versus unknown) and location (near versus far). You can't guess on this stuff, because if you have the wrong criteria, then the rest of your efforts will be wasted. So ask your market what is important to them. You can do a survey or a focus group to find those hot buttons that control consumer behavior. There are also ways to use a Customer Relationship Management system (CRM), to measure customer satisfaction or customer loyalty. If properly designed, you can learn what consumer hot buttons are based on actual purchase behavior and their feedback.

2. Survey your market. Once you've identified consumer hot buttons, you need to find out how consumers rate your products, as well as how they rate your competitors. My preferred way of doing this is to have consumers identify competing products, then rate them based on hot button criteria. It's also good to get core customer demo-

graphics and psychographic information to see if there might be some segmentation value i.e. different segments generate different maps and you can use this to reach the segments better with unique brand offerings.

3. Graph the results. Computer programs can make this a lot easier and if you've got more than two dimensions you want to graph, computers are necessary. You can use Excel to do this, although there is special software for perceptual mapping and you can buy other statistical and analysis software like Tableau, which is more expensive, but can be used for lots of analysis projects. If you have to, do it manually in PowerPoint. Regardless, the map should not only display the position of various brands, but the size of the brand on the map should reflect its market share (so you'll need to gather this info from secondary sources).

4. Interpret the perceptual map. This step is where you get strategic brand value from the map. Here are some things to look for on your map.

Do consumer attitudes toward my brand match what I want them to think about my brand?

Do consumer attitudes toward my competitors match what I thought about them?

Who are the competitors that consumers see as closest to my brand?

Are there gaps in the map indicating a potential for new brands?

Make changes in your brand or marketing strategy. If consumers don't see your brand in a favorable way, you need to make changes. If there's really something wrong with your brand leading to poor consumer attitudes, then fix your brand. If not, changes to your messaging and marketing campaign are needed to help moderate these attitudes. If consumers view competitors as being very similar to your brand, think about how your brand can stand out. You really don't want to go head-to-head with competitors and price is the last tool you should use to differentiate your brand. If there are gaps you think represent viable products that your company can produce, think about introducing a new product, a new sub-brand or moving your brand into the unfilled position.

CRAFTING YOUR BRAND STRATEGY

In a situation where you're selling to multiple personalities within a target segment, it's best to first connect everyone on common ground and then articulate clearly what's in it for each of them. The goal is to stimulate an engaging conversation that allows you to change perception, set expectations and bring clarity to the conversation. That's the essence of developing a brand strategy. The foundation of your marketing communications actually builds authentic relationships between you and your target audience. It is defining your brand strategy first that allows you to utilize marketing, advertising, public relations and social media to consistently and accurately reinforce your character. Without defining the core brand strategy, all channels of marketing communication can often become a hit and miss expense. Don't "spray and pray."

Here are 10 brand strategy principles I believe to be the key in achieving both business and marketing success.

Define your brand. It starts with your authenticity, the core purpose, vision, mission, position, values and character. Focus on what you do best and then communicate your inimitable strengths through consistency. There are many examples of companies acquiring other brands only to sell them off later because they don't fit within the brand and its architecture.

Your brand is your business model. Support and challenge your business model to maximize the potential within your brand. Think about Dollar Shave Club and how they set out to lower the price of razors and simplify shaving. That also matched their strategy of selling directly to their customers via their subscription based business model.

Consistency, consistency, consistency. Consistency in your message is the key to differentiate your brand in the market pool. Own your position on every reference point for everything that you do. Nike tells you to "Just do it" and BMW has always been known as the "ultimate driving machine."

Start from the inside out. Everyone in your company can tell you what they see, think and feel about your brand. That's the story you should bring to the customers as well, drive impact beyond just the walls of marketing. As an example, look at how Zappos empowers its employees to strengthen consumer perception on its brand by allowing them to solve customer problems on their own without supervisor approval.

Connect on the emotional level. A brand is not a name, logo, website, ad campaign or PR; those are only the tactical marketing tools not the brand. A brand is a desirable idea manifested in products, services, people, places and experiences. Starbucks created a third space experience that's desirable and exclusive so people would want to stay and pay for the over-priced coffee. Sell people something that satisfies not only their physical needs but their emotional needs and their need to identify themselves to your brand.

Empower brand champions. Reward those that love your brand, customers or employees, to help drive the message, facility activities so they can be part of the process. If your brand advocate doesn't tell you what you should or should not be doing, it's time to evaluate your brand promise. Go and talk to someone that works at the Apple retail store or an iPhone owner and you'll see just how passionate they are about Apple. The Apple brand to them is a lifestyle and a culture.

Stay relevant and flexible. A well-managed brand is always making adjustments. Branding is a process, not a race nor an event so expect to constantly tweak your message and refresh your image. Successful brands don't cling to the old ways just because they worked in the past; instead, they try to re-invent themselves by being flexible which frees them to be more savvy and creative.

Align tactics with strategy. Convey the brand message on the most appropriate media platform with specific campaign objectives. Because consumers are bombarded by commercial messages every day, they're also actively blocking out the great majority of them. Invest your branding efforts on the right platform that communicates to customers via the right channels.

Measure the effectiveness. Focus on the ROI (return on investment) is the key to measure the effectiveness of your strategies. Often times it is how well your organization can be inspired to execute the strategies. It could also be reflected in brand valuation or how your customers react to your product and price adjustments. Ultimately it should resonate with sales (and repeat sales) and that means profitability. But don't just focus on increasing sales when you could be getting a profit boost by reducing overhead and expenses as well. Give yourself options to test different marketing tactics, make sure they fit your brand authenticity and align with your strategy.

Cultivate your community. Community is a powerful and effective platform on which to engage customers and create loyalty towards the brand. In an active community, members feel a need to connect with each other in the context of the brand's consumption. Brand communities allow companies to collaborate with customers in all phases of value creation via crowd-sourcing such as product design, pricing strategy, availability, and even where to offer the product or service.

WHATEVER YOUR BRAND STRATEGY, BETTER BE AUTHENTIC

Regardless of your brand strategy, 'authenticity' is an aspect of branding that's important to consider in order to be relevant in today's marketplaces. Brand authenticity is not a trendy marketing buzzword. In its most simple sense, brand authenticity means honesty. Layer transparency and integrity onto that, and you have a business approach that is as rooted in reality as it is inspired. There is already authenticity at work in every business or organization. It is the set of core beliefs that drives the brand and the activity. It's the stuff that just happens, naturally and truthfully. No pretending, no falsehoods, no saying your brand is something that it isn't, or stands for something that it doesn't. *Authenticity is the glass wall at the sausage factory.* Are you cool with what consumers will see when they look into your world? Are you excited to share it with them?

When you really think about it, authenticity comes down to giving people a reason to care. Consumers want to care - they want to believe that their purchase is making a difference somewhere, somehow, and that the brands they are supporting with their hard-earned dollars are living out the values that they believe in. People respond to honesty, integrity, enthusiasm and love, and they can spot frauds a mile away. It's never too late to look for the authenticity that exists within your business and to capitalize on it with thoughtful, engaging marketing campaigns.

BRAND INSIGHT

This company got its start in 2002 when the company founder was trying to solve a simple problem but could not find a solution in the marketplace. So he created one. Initially the product was intended for serious action sports enthusiasts, a fun crowd but a relatively small target segment. Little did the company know just how much another trend, social media, would explode the popularity of its product. With the rise of social media, everyone was capturing images and video and sharing them online. The company's sales grew rapidly and they focused on product marketing to fuel sales. But with the rise of social media, came the evolution of smartphones with better and better cameras. Now GoPro was in trouble. They had built a "product" based brand and not really crafted a strong emotional connection to their customers. Those customers were now leaving in droves. New potential customers saw no reason to buy a GoPro. Customers might have purchased their GoPro to takes photos and videos but obviously, they did not "love" their GoPro.

KEY TAKEAWAY

You better define and build your brand strategy from the beginning to create an emotional connection to your customers. You better be ready to adjust your products features or services when competition arrives. If not, you will be relegated to selling just a product. And products are way harder to defend and protect than brands.

CHAPTER SIX
TEN BRAND BUILDING STRATEGIES.
* * *

If you talk to several young digital marketers, they will say that building a strong brand entails creating a cool name, maybe a creative logo, then advertising and marketing that brand to potential buyers, and enforcing brand message consistency in all customer interactions. However, they would be wrong. Brand marketing can neither create nor build nor strengthen a brand. The brand is always a reflection of the quality of the product or service. If you build a "piece of shit", regardless of the amount of branding or creativity in the marketing, it's still a piece of shit. There are no exceptions to this law of branding. As a matter of fact, doing great marketing with a weak product will kill it faster than if you did no marketing.

To understand why this is the case, its first necessary to get a deeper understanding of "brand." Most people think a brand consists of exterior elements: the brand name, the logo, the tag line, and the associated marketing. Thinking of a brand like this, however, is like thinking of your significant other as a collection of skin, clothes, and utterances. The essence of a brand is not the exterior elements, but how you feel about the product or service. It's what's inside. The purpose of the brand elements is not to create those feelings, but to remind you of them. If your feelings about the product are negative, those brand elements simply remind you of how much you dislike the product.

Your brand is like a bank account. When you delight customers, it adds value to the brand. If you have a string of great products, customers will forget the occasional flop. Apple is a case in point. Few people remember that they've had some real stinkers. I personally worked on a product launch to support Newton, an Apple PDA (personal digital assistant) like product. The problem was no one could really define it. Worse, the handwriting recognition software had serious bugs. It failed miserably. But Apple marched on. That is the power of a brand. So when you irritate customers, it extracts value from the brand, and eventually you end up overdrawn and even if you change your ways and come out with some great products, it may take years, if ever, for customers to forget the taint.

The only way to build a strong brand is to create and sell a product or service that delights your customers. If you fail at this basic step, brand marketing is not just a waste of money, but actively counterproductive. Therefore, if you want to build a strong brand, put your time and money into creating and selling the best product or service possible. Then, if you've got some left over, use brand marketing to help spread the word. But before you do brand strategy or marketing, let's review what I call the brand "rainbow."

UNDERSTANDING THE BRAND RAINBOW

Creating a brand is hard work. If it was easy everyone would have great brands. The reality is most companies create products, not brands. Today's marketers just want to move faster and get it done now. Crafting a great brand without sounding "artsy fartsy" is putting in the time and attention to actually building something great. Do you want to go to a restaurant that has an okay chef or a top chef? So that you have a clear understanding of the "stages" of brand development and some of the steps needed, let me walk you through the "rainbow" of brand development. Here are my five stages of a brand rainbow.

BRAND AUDIT: This is the first step that really sets the stage for the creation of the brand. Here is what's important:

Company mission and vision

Company culture and values

Customer experience & satisfaction goals

Sales process (intended)

Key products and or services

Market environment

Competitor landscape

Research and analysis

BRAND RAINBOW

BRAND INSIGHT: This is where you really set the values of the brand, determine the key differentiator (s) and look at your competitive advantage.

Core brand values

Brand attributes

Brand strengths and weaknesses

Opportunities and threats

Future casting (look forward five years)

Business category

Industry health

Target segment defined (who are the initial customers)

Brand differentiators

Key competitive advantage

BRAND POSITION: This probably forms the very core of the brand and its unique position in the marketplace. Done well, this is makes customers "feel" something of value in your brand.

Unique value proposition

Who are we to our target audience?

Why is that important?

What is our brand position?

What do we want customers to say or feel?

BRAND CREATION: These are the most visual elements of the brand; this is where great creativity and a unique promise create the brand image.

Name of the brand

Design of logo and identity

Create the narrative and personality

Create the tone and voice

Visual palette, colors, graphic standards, imagery

Key messages

BRAND COMMUNICATIONS: This is what most people think marketing is, that is, all the marketing tactics to either inform or sell something. Just anchor it in the brand.

Customer experience

Employee behavior

Brand manifesto

Brand signage (i.e. stationary, signage, wayfinding, etc.)

Product or service packaging

Marketing campaign elements (i.e. mobile, online, offline, etc.)

Word of mouth

Brand manual (i.e. guidelines, identity, voice, persona, etc.)

The one element that really ties a brand together and gives it its originating core is the brand story. We have all met people who have started companies that have become brands. And when they tell us how it all got started we are amazed. So, understanding how to tell a brand story is critical.

THE ART OF CRAFTING AND TELLING A BRAND STORY

What is a brand story? A brand story is more than content and a narrative. The story goes beyond what's written in the copy on a website, the text in a brochure or the presentation used to pitch to investors or customers. Your story isn't just what you tell people, it's also what they believe about you based on the signals your brand sends. The story is a complete picture made up of facts, feelings and interpretations, which means that part of your story isn't even told by you. Everything you do, each element of your business or brand, from the colors and texture of your packaging and business cards, to the staff you hire is part of your brand story and every element should reflect the truth about your brand back to your audience. If you want to build a successful, sustainable business and a brand that will garner loyalty, and if you're lucky, become loved, you have to start with your story.

Why do you need a brand story? If you don't have a story you are just another commodity. A replaceable cog in the consumer consumption machine. You have no way to differentiate your brand or your business. Creating a brand story is not simply about standing out and getting noticed. It's about building something that people care about and want to buy into. It's about relating to your audience and being human. It's about framing your scarcity and dictating your value. It's about thinking beyond the utility and functionality of products and services and striving for the creation of loyalty and meaningful bonds with your customers. A brand story is not just a catchy tagline that's pasted on a billboard to attract attention for a week or two. Your story is the foundation of your brand and a strategy for future growth.

A brand story is how Starbucks created a whole new coffee category and elevated itself above its competitors. That story is the reason people drive further, passing Dunkin Donuts and 7 Eleven on the way to pay two times more for a cup of coffee every morning.

Think about the story of how Steve Jobs and Steve Wozniak started Apple in a garage. Or how FedEx got its initial start via an economics paper by then student Fred Smith. Brands like Starbucks, Apple and FedEx are built on so much more than the utility and specifications of their products. Your product is only part of the story. A potential customer's relationship with your brand will likely begin before they actually purchase your product at all.

Your story begins with the connection made when the customer hears your name for the first time, when he/she sees your logo, visits your website, reads your website "about us" page and experiences your interactions on social media. The signals you send about not just what you do and how well you do it, but about what you stand for, build the complete picture of your brand. Marketing often happens when you are not listening and your customer is telling a friend how your product changed his/her life. So know your story and then craft the right brand strategy.

10 STRATEGIES FOR BUILDING A BRAND

A branding strategy helps establish a product within the market and to build a brand that will grow and mature in a saturated or even growing marketplace. Making smart branding decisions up front is crucial since a company may have to live with the decision for a long time. The following are commonly used branding strategies:

COMPANY NAME. In this case a strong brand name (or company name) is made the vehicle for a range of products (for example, Mercedes Benz or Black & Decker) or a range of subsidiary brands like YUM Foods which owns Taco Bell, KFC and Pizza Hut.

INDIVIDUAL BRANDING. Each brand has a separate name, putting it into a de facto competition against other brands from the same company (for example, Kool-Aid and Tang are both owned by Kraft Foods). Individual brand names naturally allow greater flexibility by permitting a variety of different products, of differing quality, to be sold without confusing the consumer's perception of what business the company is in or diluting higher quality products.

ATTITUDE BRANDING AND ICONIC BRANDS. This is the choice to represent a larger feeling, which is not necessarily connected with the product or consumption of the product at all. Companies that use attitude branding include: Nike, Starbucks, The Body Shop, and Apple, Inc. Iconic brands are defined as having aspects that contribute to the consumer's self-expression and personal identity.

BRAND IDENTITY VALUE. Brands whose value to consumers comes primarily from having identity value are said to be "identity brands." Some brands have such a strong identity that they become "iconic brands" such as Apple, Nike, and Harley Davidson.

DERIVED BRANDS. Some suppliers of key components may wish to guarantee their own position by promoting that component as a brand in its own right. For example, Intel, positions itself in the PC market with the slogan (and sticker) "Intel Inside." Gore-Tex positions itself and its product formula as a protector of products through waterproofing other brands clothes.

BRAND EXTENSION AND BRAND DILUTION. The existing strong brand name can be used as a vehicle for new or modified products. For example, many fashion and designer companies extended brands into fragrances, shoes and accessories, furniture, and hotels. Frequently, the product is no different than what is already on the market, except it has a brand name marking. The risk of over-extension is brand dilution, which is when the brand loses its brand associations with a market segment, product area or quality, price, or cachet.

MULTI-BRANDS STRATEGY. Alternatively, in a very saturated market, a supplier can deliberately launch totally new brands in apparent competition with its own existing strong brand (and often with identical product characteristics) to soak up more market share. The rationale is that having 4 out of 12 brands in such a market will give a greater overall share than having 1 out of 10. Procter & Gamble is a leading exponent of this philosophy, running as many as ten detergent brands in the US market. In the hotel business, Marriott uses the name Fairfield Inns for its budget chain. Cannibalization is a particular problem of a multi-brands strategy approach, in which the new brand takes business away from an established one which the organization also owns. This may be acceptable (indeed to be expected) if there is a net gain overall.

PRIVATE LABELS. Also called own brands, or store brands, these have become increasingly popular. When the retailer has a particularly strong identity, this "own brand" may be able to compete against even the strongest brand leaders, and may outperform those products that are not otherwise strongly branded. Costco does this with its "Kirkland" brand and Trader Joes sells its own house brand throughout its stores.

INDIVIDUAL AND ORGANIZATIONAL BRANDS. These are types of branding that treat individuals and organizations as the products to be branded. Personal branding treats persons and their careers as brands. Be careful here though, because if the individual has a problem, the brand has a problem. Subways experienced this first hand.

CROWDSOURCING BRANDING. These are brands that are created by the people for the business, which is opposite to the traditional method where the business creates a brand. This type of method minimizes the risk of brand failure, since the people that might reject the brand in the traditional method are the ones who are participating in the branding process. Think of Yelp, Instagram, Craigslist, and perhaps Etsy.

MEASURE YOUR BRAND VIA A REPORT CARD

It's easy as a marketer to "fall in love" with your own branding and marketing. We have a tendency to believe in what we create. However, take a step back and evaluate your brand and marketing efforts "before" you launch. Take a critical look at what you are about to unleash. Rate your brand efforts on a scale of one to ten (one being extremely poor and ten being extremely good) for each characteristic below. Better yet, have other marketers outside your company rate your branding efforts. Then create a bar chart (visuals are always better than numbers) that reflects the scores. Use the bar chart to generate discussion among all those individuals who participate in the management of your brands. Looking at the results in that manner should help you identify areas that need improvement, recognize areas in which you excel, and learn more about how your particular brand is configured.

It can also be helpful to create a report card and chart for competitors' brands simply by rating those brands based on your own perceptions, both as a competitor and as a consumer. As an outsider, you may know more about how their brands are received in the marketplace than they do. Keep that in mind as you evaluate your own brand. Try to look at it through the eyes of consumers rather than through your own knowledge of the brand budgets, teams, and time spent on various initiatives.

- The brand excels at delivering the benefits customers truly desire.
- The brand is/has stayed relevant.
- The pricing strategy is based on consumers' perceptions of value.
- The brand is properly positioned in the marketplace.

- The brand messaging is consistent across all marketing platforms.
- The brand portfolio and hierarchy make sense.
- The brand coordinates a full repertoire of marketing activities to build equity.
- The brand's managers understand what the brand means to consumers.
- The brand is given proper support, and that support is sustained over the long run.
- The company monitors all sources of brand equity.

Most marketers will never do a brand report card. That's because most marketers do not understand branding, or worse, do not want to be held accountable for their marketing efforts if things don't turn out well. If you are doing marketing for your brand or your clients, you better live to the mantra that John Wilson, one of the co-founders of Stance, lives by: Freedom and accountability. Earn the freedom to do great marketing work but then accept the accountability for whatever happens. Good or bad.

So, take the effort to learn and understand what it takes to actually deliver on branding as a marketer. Regardless of your brand strategy, understand that it must resonate with your target audience and make them feel that you have the only solution in the marketplace for them and that there is no easy substitute for your product or service. If you don't do that, you will be the preverbal "hamster on the wheel", running all the time but never going anywhere with your brand as competitors just pick away at your market share.

BRAND INSIGHT

This company has been around for more than 100 years. In that time it has thrived and grown and it is now a household name. It crafted its brand with authenticity and originality. One of the key attributes in its product was "rocky mountain spring water." Well, the leaders at this brand wanted to leverage the growing bottled water trend in the early 1990's so they created a new product, Rocky Mountain Sparkling Water...by Coors. Instead of creating an associated or standalone brand, they branded it with the Coors logo. That was a huge mistake. Customers were confused and actually thought that it was an alcoholic drink. It failed and Coors pulled it from the market. But the water marketplace continued to grow. In 2015, bottled water sales in just the USA topped $14.2 billion.

KEY TAKEAWAY

If you build a good brand, you will have some permission to introduce other related products. If people don't believe you have the brand permission to introduce a certain product, then you don't. The solution? Create a new brand and enter a growing marketplace with all the distribution and financial resources of the core brand. You can then build a new brand while preserving the core brand.

CHAPTER SEVEN
BRAND ARCHITECTURE AND DECISION TREES.
✱ ✱ ✱

If you are under the age of 35 and are a digital marketer, do you ever feel you just don't get the respect you deserve especially as you move upstream and work with larger brands? In those moments, do you ever feel like the actor Joe Pesci in the movie Good Fellas when he is in the midst of a heated conversation with a fellow gangster and utters the memorable line," You think I'm funny? I'm funny how, I mean funny, like I'm a clown?" As a digital marketer, you probably don't know what you don't know about brand architecture and decision trees. Brands and clients want people that can push or guide them strategically. If you are not strategic, then you won't get the respect you feel you deserve. Well, there is good news. When I started my marketing career, I did not understand brand architecture or decision trees at all. I did not understand branding. I just assumed marketing naturally worked its way out. That could not be further from the truth.

The whole concept of brand management is that the company and its executives are in total control of their brand(s) and, to some degree, get to architect, design and implement their brands into the marketplace. Brands are placed into every marketplace by design or default. Let me give you a simple example of brand architecture so that you understand what I am talking about. Let's take General Motors, the automotive company and one of their products:

Master brand: General Motors

Sub brand: Chevrolet

Model brand: Corvette

Product brand: Grand Sport

In this simple example, this is the brand architecture and related hierarchy. Every brand has some form of brand hierarchy. The more you understand this, the more you start to become a more strategic marketer when it comes to branding. Why? Because this simple explanation does not even begin to scratch the surface of branding. When you mix in disrupted industries, changing marketplaces, varied population segments and competitors, all of sudden it can get really complicated.

UNDERSTANDING BRAND ARCHITECTURE TODAY

A better understanding and more expansive view of brand architecture is needed today, especially for digital marketers. Brand experts and authors such as David Aaker and Kevin Lane Keller put the topic of brand architecture on the map and gave us useful language and frameworks for organizing brands in their books on branding. The most widely used of these terms include "house of brands" (e.g. Proctor and Gamble (P & G) with their many product brands that have little to no linkage to the corporate brand) and "branded house" (e.g. General Electric (GE) with their diversified businesses all falling under the GE master brand. While helpful in establishing approaches toward architecting portfolios of brands, these early definitions fall short of addressing the issues today's companies face. In my marketing career working with companies like Apple, Visa, American Express, etc. on key branding decisions, I have found that as soon as brand architecture issues are raised, the dialogue quickly moves into directions ranging from extremely strategic (how do I organize my go-to-market businesses?) to extremely tactical (what should I name product / service X?). If brand architecture is a structure for organizing brands in a portfolio to achieve some benefit for a company, then both the very strategic and very tactical elements should be considered. Extending to more strategic decisions "what to brand vs. what not to brand" is a key question all organizations and marketers must ask before defining their brand architecture, as the answer has significant implications relative to resources and go-to-market strategies.

Let me give you another example that might make all of this make sense. You are the chief marketing officer at Kellogg's in the year 2000. You have been watching and researching the market and notice changing habits in the consumer marketplace. People are eating healthier. At the time, Kellogg's is making cereal for mostly children, lots of sugars, not necessarily healthy. Then the CEO walks into your office and says, "We just bought Kashi." So as the head of marketing, what do you do? Here are some of your branding options:

> Create a healthy line of Kellogg's adult cereal?
>
> Change the name of Kashi to Kellogg's?
>
> Endorse the Kashi brand with Kellogg's ownership?
>
> Leave Kashi as a standalone brand and fund its growth?

Now, are you beginning to see the key importance of understanding branding, brand architecture and even brand portfolio management? Let's review brand portfolio management and then I will tell you what Kellogg's did and why.

BRAND PORTFOLIO STRATEGY QUESTIONS

As you move up in your career of marketing or start to really grow your strategic marketing expertise, you really need to understand branding, brand architecture and how all of that relates to marketing. With respect to the Kellogg's example, you could ask yourself these questions:

What specifically is the brand charged with doing for the Company? What objectives should be set for the brand from a volume and financial perspective? What role does/should the brand serve from a channel perspective? What are the optimal pricing structures and price points for the brand? What sort of price differential should exist between it and its most direct competitors? What sort of promotional support should the brand receive?

How should the brand be positioned to the consumer, taking into consideration its strategic role within the portfolio, consumer wants/needs, and its current equities? What is (or should be) its unique point of difference?

What is the brand's contribution to the Master Brand proposition? To what extent does it help the Company deliver on its brand promises? Does the brand help the Company reinforce desirable equities?

BRAND PORTFOLIO STRATEGY

What is the optimal relationship between the product brand and the Company brand? Should there be an explicit relationship between it and other brands within the brand portfolio? If yes, what is the best way to establish this linkage?

What is the brand's "bounds of extendibility?" From a category perspective, where can the brand credibly go today, or in the near term or intermediate future? What should be considered off-limits for the brand?

I worked with Kellogg's early in my marketing career and had no clue about branding or brand architecture. However, with my mentors and my increased role in strategic marketing, I became a brand expert after about seven years. A brand expert has the capability of walking into any conference room for any company, and while he/she does not yet have the answers, *they absolutely know the right questions to ask.*

Now, with respect to the Kellogg's example above, what would you do? Do you create a line of healthy adult cereal by Kellogg's? No, for two reasons. Kashi is a highly respected brand already focused on healthy adult cereal. And Kellogg's has a reputation of sugar based cereal for children. If Kellogg's introduced a line of cereal like this, it would not be believable and would actually hurt the Kellogg's brand. You don't change the brand Kashi to Kellogg's for the same reasons. Do you endorse the Kellogg's brand name to Kashi (e.g. Kashi, a Kellogg's Company)? What value would that create? Not much. While the Kellogg's brand is valuable, not so much as it relates to healthy cereal. So, you chose the last branding option. Leave Kashi as a free standing brand that you will grow with all the financial and distribution resources of Kellogg's. That is what Kellogg's did and they almost screwed that up. For a period of time they moved Kashi employees to Battle Creek, Michigan from California and sales fell almost 30 percent. Kellogg's tried to force its conservative brand management and culture on a brand that was more free-spirited and open. Almost killed it. Luckily, a few years ago, Kellogg's realized its mistake and moved Kashi back to Southern California and they seem to be flourishing again. The key lesson is to understand that the consumer gets to decide what you do with a brand so make the right decision with your target audience in mind. Ignore them at your peril.

LEFT OR RIGHT? BRAND DECISION MAKING

By now, you should be starting to understand that if you want to build your marketing career, you better become a branding expert. What's the difference between a really good marketing person and a brand expert? Millions. When our agency was asked to review a brand or create a new brand, we got paid millions just to do the brand analysis and provide strategic recommendations. The reason is that for some companies, billions was at stake. A wrong decision could cost a company billions in lost revenue or it could kill an entire division of the company. So, you need to make your brand decisions with a good brand analysis, review the brand architecture, understand the competition and most importantly, understand the customer.

To continue your learning about branding, let me share with you some companies and their branding decisions.

COCA COLA: ENTER NEW MARKETS. As soda sales started to decline and consumers were drinking healthier alternatives like water, Coca Cola was faced with making an important decision. That decision was spurred by the launch of Aquafina by rival Pepsi. In short order Coca Cola decided to create a new water brand, not related to the Coca Cola brand. Using filtered tap water, they created Dasani and built the brand with their resources. Later they also bought Vitamin Water. Cocoa Cola's brand did not have the consumer or brand permission to create Coca Cola water. Consumers would simply not have believed in it. Most consumers don't know that Coca Cola owns Dasani and Vitamin Water.

STARBUCKS: ADD MORE VALUE. As Starbucks created their brand around being the "third place" to hang out, after home and work, they played close attention to changing consumer needs. As they noticed more people drinking tea, they bought Tazo. Then they noticed people drinking tea but not at Starbucks. So they bought Tevana, a brand that sold tea but also had its own stores. Today Tevana has grown to a large tea house brand and Tazo is still doing fine as a tea brand. For both brands, they pretty much stand-alone with their own branding. If you search closely, you will see they are both owned by Starbucks. Starbucks did such a great job branding itself around coffee, they did not believe they could create a tea brand.

PROCTOR AND GAMBLE: OWN THE SHELF. P & G made a strategic decision years ago that would drive its "house of brands" strategy. That is, they wanted to build a dominant company but not a dominate brand. They wanted the ability to create multiple brands for the "shelf" in the store aisle and did not really care which one you bought as long as you bought one of their brands. That is why today, they own Tide, Ariel and Gain laundry detergents. It's why they own Crest and Oral-B. Most consumers do not know that one company owns these brands and perhaps that does not matter as long as the product brand is awesome. With this strategy they can build or buy brands into infinity to meet changing consumer demands.

APPLE: EXPERTISE WITHOUT RISK. I will be honest with you. I still don't understand the acquisition of Beats by Apple. To me, and a lot of critics, the Beats headphones were more of a fashion statement than a technically advanced set of headphones. I think Apple is a smart company so they must have acquired the company to get the founders and perhaps something else. Anyway, if you look at Beats today, it does not carry any Apple branding. That is because Apple wanted to minimize its risk associated with the acquisition. If Beats failed or the founders did something untoward, nothing would reflect back on the Apple brand.

BUDWEISER: CRAFT NEW BRANDS. What do you do if you're the "king of beers" and people stop buying your product? What if your brand is associated with an older target segment? If you are Budweiser, you leverage a growing trend by buying craft beer companies. And Budweiser has been doing just that for more than 20 years. As regular beer sales continue to decline, big beer brands have only two choices. Create a craft beer brand or buy one. In Budweiser's case, it's actually cheaper to buy the rising craft brands. They are in fact creating, just like P & G, a "house of craft brands" that will be attractive to a variety of craft beer drinkers. Widmer, RedHook, Goose Island and Kona Brewing, to name a few, are all owned by Budweiser. With the rise of craft beer into the foreseeable future, it is really the only strategy that Budweiser has as its core brand becomes less relevant.

BRAND DECISIONS DO GROW ON TREES

The first time I saw a brand decision tree, I was amazed that some critical brand decisions could be explored via a decision making tree. The really powerful benefits of a brand decision tree, other than making good informed decisions, are the following: it creates a visual diagram of possible choices, eliminates random barnstorming opinions, clearly lays out the pros and cons of each option, can be easily customized and almost clinically presents you with the best option in your branding strategy. In a few pages, I will show you an example of a brand decision tree we used to use at our agency.

These decision trees typically deal with branding issues such as:

>How should we name a new product or service?

>Should we keep an acquisition's brand identity?

>Should we endorse a company or offering with our parent name?

>Should we have a separate logo?

>How should we identify a joint venture or other similar arrangement?

Decision trees help to remove some of the subjectivity. Particularly with naming and other brand identity issues, there are often conflicting points of view within an organization. Typically, a corporate brand manager might want to reduce the number of brands and logos being used throughout the company while a particular product manager might want a cool, new brand for his or her new offering. With a decision tree, the brand manager can say "sure you can have a cool brand name," but first make a business case by answering the questions in the brand decision tree. Brand decision trees provide a streamlined process to help make strategic decisions, which have an impact on your brand. However, the reality is that they're only useful when management mandates their use, builds them into internal processes and rewards successful applications.

While every organization's brand decision tree is different, the fundamental questions that any brand decision making tree should answer should include the following:

> Is the product or service unique?
>
> Does the product or service enhance or support the master brand?
>
> Does it strengthen master brand equity?
>
> Would it weaken our master brand?
>
> Is it strategically important for the growth of the company in the future?
>
> Is there a high level of risk associated with the new product or service?

These are some of the questions that you need to answer before you get an itch to create a "logo" for a new brand product or service. Remember, a logo is a graphic representation of your company or brand. This is only one small part of your brand strategy. You could even argue it's the *least* important part of your brand strategy. Before you move into the logo identity design phase, be sure to identify your brand positioning and value proposition. If you're having a difficult time defining those two things, then you may have just saved yourself, and your designer, a lot of time and money.

DESIGN AND USE OF A BRAND DECISION TREE

In order to better understand the creation and use of a brand decision tree, I have created one for you. I will use the fictitious company name and brand "Newco" as I construct the decision tree. Let's assume we are either going to create or acquire a new product line. As you can see from the brand decision tree example below, there are a set of simple but important questions, that when answered, lead to a suggested brand recommendation. Let's review a simple brand decision tree:

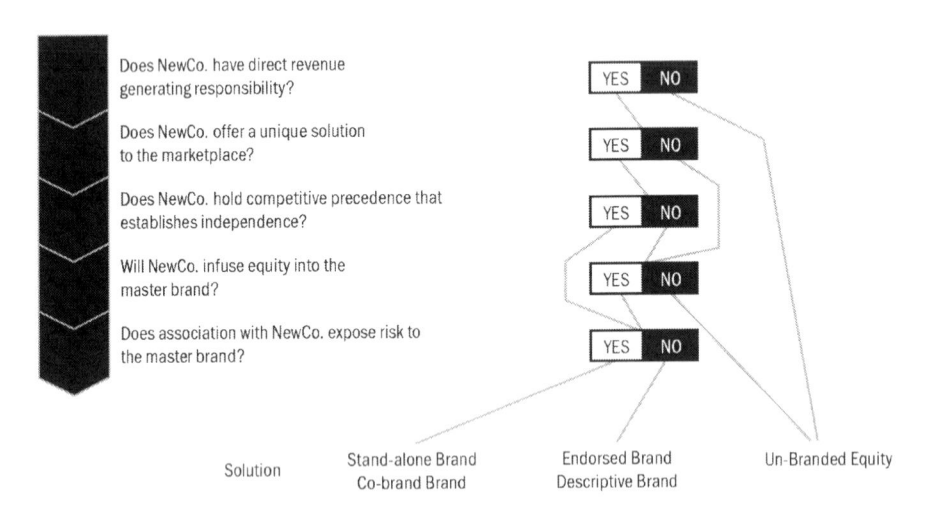

Does NewCo. have direct revenue generating responsibility? YES NO

Does NewCo. offer a unique solution to the marketplace? YES NO

Does NewCo. hold competitive precedence that establishes independence? YES NO

Will NewCo. infuse equity into the master brand? YES NO

Does association with NewCo. expose risk to the master brand? YES NO

Solution | Stand-alone Brand / Co-brand Brand | Endorsed Brand / Descriptive Brand | Un-Branded Equity

BRAND DECISION TREE

While this is a very simple brand decision tree, you can look at the example and start to understand the clinical approach and why this methodology could be a very powerful tool when making decisions about branding. Imagine you are working with a brand that makes market leading oatmeal and has a great brand reputation built over 50 years. The company executives tell you they want to move into the "juice or yogurt" categories by either acquiring companies or creating new product lines. What is your branding recommendation? Would their brand be believable in those categories? Do you need to create or buy new brands? You can't make this kind of decision based on intuition or gut feeling. You better do a clinical brand tree analysis that everyone can understand and clearly see the pros and cons of every branding option. See the example of a branding tree we used in our agency.

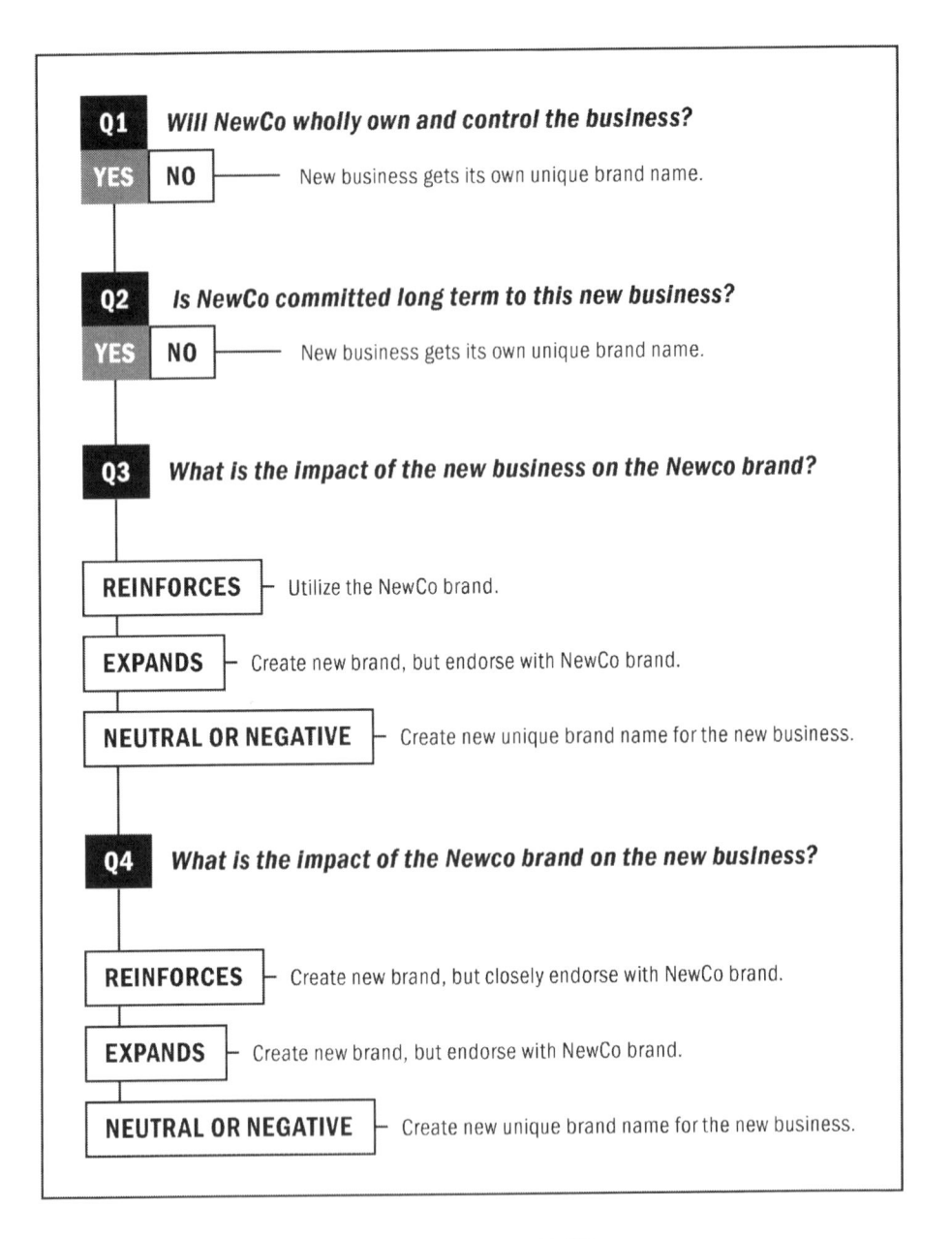

Q1 *Will NewCo wholly own and control the business?*

YES | NO —— New business gets its own unique brand name.

Q2 *Is NewCo committed long term to this new business?*

YES | NO —— New business gets its own unique brand name.

Q3 *What is the impact of the new business on the Newco brand?*

- **REINFORCES** — Utilize the NewCo brand.
- **EXPANDS** — Create new brand, but endorse with NewCo brand.
- **NEUTRAL OR NEGATIVE** — Create new unique brand name for the new business.

Q4 *What is the impact of the Newco brand on the new business?*

- **REINFORCES** — Create new brand, but closely endorse with NewCo brand.
- **EXPANDS** — Create new brand, but endorse with NewCo brand.
- **NEUTRAL OR NEGATIVE** — Create new unique brand name for the new business.

BRAND DECISION TREE

In all my years of doing branding work, most marketers I meet do not really understand branding at a deep strategic level. No Millennial digital marketer I have ever met has convinced me they could walk into a $3 billion brand and understand what to do from a strategic perspective. Harsh comment from me but I am speaking from experience. They may understand brandings' purpose and role but they don't know how to do it. If you are a digital marketer today and you wonder why you are not getting invited to the "big party" dance for major brands or large agencies, they just don't see you as a strategic marketer. The good news is that you can learn exactly what it takes to become a branding expert and understanding brand architecture and utilizing brand decision trees will help you immensely. If nothing else, it helps you to understand the kind of simple questions you should be asking in strategic brand meetings.

BRAND INSIGHT

This company was once the undisputed leader in smartphones. It's early rise and secure solutions were industry leading. And its brand name was very powerful in several customer segments. But eventually it started to fail. So what happened? The reason they failed provides a prime example of an incumbent business being disrupted by sprightlier newcomers. Success for this brand bred three interrelated negatives: conservatism, complacency and arrogance. The senior executives remarked when asked about the initial Apple iPhone introduction in 2007, "It wasn't secure, it had rapid battery drain and a lousy "digital" keyboard. "It's OK, we'll be fine." The lesson learned? Brands live and die by their customers and when BlackBerry did not evolve to meet customer demands and expectations of smartphones, the marketplace continued to grow as BlackBerry failed.

KEY TAKEAWAY

If you are fortunate enough to be a brand that is a market leader, you better pay attention to your competition and focus on delivering value to your current, and more importantly, your future customers. Because if you don't another brand will be happy to take your customers. And, no matter your success, never be arrogant. It only works in Quentin Tarantino movies.

CHAPTER EIGHT
THE ART OF POSITIONING A BRAND.
* * *

Many people have different interpretations about what brand positioning means. It's one of those concepts that is hard to pin down, yet at the same time is so important to the success of your brand. Positioning is at the heart of your brand strategy. It's essentially the summation of everything your brand is about. Marty Neumeier who wrote the Brand Gap says that a brand is not what YOU say it is. It's what THEY say it is. They being the customer. This is a concept most marketers can't get their head around. Think about it this way, when you think of a car rental company, what brand pops into your head? Hertz? Enterprise? Budget? Today, it might even be Uber. These brands popping into your head for almost any product or service are not an accident. They were placed there by the brand we associate with or through our experiences. Pretty mystical, eh? Actually, it's not mysterious; it's more of a science. So let me try and explain it to you.

Your brand positioning is built from what you know to be true about your customer. It takes the benefits of your product or service that you've outlined and makes them meaningful to customers. In its simplest of forms, positioning is the mental space you want to occupy in your customer's mind. It's the first thing you want your customer to think about when they hear your brand name. You say "smart hydration", your customer says, "SmartWater." In good brand positioning, you want to add emotion into the product benefit mix because you want your customer to "feel" something. How you build an emotional connection with your customer is the key to being a powerful brand. But that emotional bond should be reflected in the positioning statement for the business. Positioning is more about em0tions and less about the facts. That's why marketers, who think a claim about their product or service is a positioning statement, really miss the boat. The same goes for a description of your type of business. There's no emotion in that and yet it's emotions that differentiate a brand. Nike does not position or create emotion around a product feature, they say, "Just do it."

I remember when we created our own agency, CKS|Partners. As a team we were working on how we wanted to position our "*integrated marketing agency*", looking for the emotional benefit that we could offer to our clients. We finally landed on *"our integrated brand marketing expertise will make your brand more powerful and get you promoted"* as our positioning. We never used it as a tagline, but more as a positioning statement for how we would serve up what we offered clients. Our actual positioning words to the customer were,"CKS|Partners helps build powerful brands through an *integrated marketing* discipline." Again we never had a tagline. But all of our branding and marketing was done to reinforce and convey the emotional benefit of our positioning. We had to have our clients believe that the *synergy* of integrated marketing would do more for less money and that we would create a more powerful marketing campaign based on brand strategy. And that success would get them promoted. It must have worked because in less than six years, we became the leading integrated marketing agency in the world with $1.2 billion in revenue, 10,000 employees and offices in 30 countries.

Once it's nailed, your brand's positioning becomes the basis for building the brand experience across the entire marketing plan. The key is to make sure the actual brand experience delivers on what was intended in the positioning. You need to find the right brand positioning that helps create the emotional benefit that you offer your customer. Think about how you want your customer to feel about you, every time they think about your brand.

WHY IS BRAND POSITIONING IMPORTANT?

Brands that are well positioned occupy particular niches in consumers' minds. They are similar to and different from competing brands in certain reliably identifiable ways. The most successful brands in this regard keep up with competitors by creating points of parity in those areas where competitors are trying to find an advantage while at the same time creating points of difference to achieve advantages over competitors in some other areas. The Mercedes-Benz and Apple brands, for example, hold clear advantages in product design and performance and match competitors level of product innovation and service. Ritz Carlton and Nordstrom lead their respective packs in customer service and hold their own in quality. Levi's and Harley-Davidson excel at providing compelling user and usage imagery while offering adequate or even strong performance of their products.

Visa is a particularly good example of a brand whose managers understand the power of brand positioning. In the 1970s and 1980s, American Express maintained the high-profile brand in the credit card market through a series of highly effective marketing programs. Trumpeting that "*membership has its privileges*," American Express came to signify status, prestige and quality. In response, Visa introduced the Gold and the Platinum cards and launched an aggressive marketing campaign to build up the status of its cards to match the American Express cards. It also developed an extensive merchant delivery system to differentiate itself on the basis of superior convenience and accessibility. Its ad campaigns showcased desirable locations such as famous restaurants, resorts and events that *did not accept* American Express while proclaiming, "*Visa. It's everywhere you want to be.*" The aspirational message cleverly reinforced both accessibility and prestige and helped Visa stake out a formidable position for its brand. Visa became the consumer card of choice for family and personal shopping, for personal travel and entertainment, and even for international travel, a former American Express stronghold. Of course, branding isn't static, and brand positioning is even more difficult when a brand spans many product categories. The mix of points of parity and point of difference that works for a brand in one category may not be quite right for the same brand in another category. In the end, customers get to decide but you can help.

DEFINING THE CONCEPT OF "POSITIONING" IN MARKETING

The term "positioning" really came to life in an article on the subject published by Jack Trout in 1969. In 1972, Al Ries and Jack Trout published a series of articles on the topic in Advertising Age. But it was Ries and Trout's 1981 bestselling book, *Positioning: The Battle for Your Mind*, which firmly established and popularized the concept in the advertising world. The breakthrough part of Ries and Trout's conceptualization is that "*a positioning*" exists only in the mind of the customer. Ries and Trout felt that, in an era of information overload, which at the time was driven by continuous streams of advertising messages, the consumer would only be able to accept and absorb those messages consistent with prior knowledge or experience. Positioning would help the advertiser break through the message clutter. So, good positioning presents a simplified message consistent with what the consumer already believes by focusing on the perceptions of the consumer, rather than on the reality of the product.

The idea that consumer perceptions are critical to the success of a product changed the very basis on which new products could be developed. In their 1987 article entitled "*Psychological Meaning of Products and Product Positioning,*" Friedmann and Lessig, two university marketing professors, argued that products can engender important psychological meaning to customers, and that these psychological meanings can be both complementary and convergent from differentiation strategies based only on rational product attributes.

The concept of positioning has been embraced by the marketing expert mainstream, with the vast majority of marketers using the term as part of their professional lexicon. The term "positioning" has evolved (or devolved, depending on one's point of view) generally to describe any number of techniques by which marketers try to create an image or identity for a product, brand, or company in the mind of a target audience.

Popular tools to assess brand positioning include graphical perceptual mapping, market surveys, and certain statistical techniques. Marketing strategists have layered, expanded, and refined elements in the concept of "positioning." Researchers have created a plethora of techniques to measure "positioning." Yet, in the end what matters is how potential buyers perceive the product as it is expressed relative to the position of competition. Today, however, the digital marketing community seems to have lost the simple importance of the original "positioning" philosophy. In the digital marketing age of "implement fast, ask questions later" marketing, this is a mistake. Another key concept of positioning, category ladders, is a key component of brand positioning.

EXPERT POSITIONING: CHOOSE YOUR LADDER WISELY

Earlier in this chapter, I talked about what pops into your mind when I referenced car rental companies. Usually it's three to four brands and that's not an accident. You see, as humans, we tend to categorize products and brands neatly in our mind into categories. It just helps us organize what we believe. We also utilize a "ladder" in each one of our categories. So, understand that these "category ladders" are in everyone's mind for every product category. Well, if your brand can't get into the top three or four for each category ladder in your customers mind, then you have a problem. You do have a couple of choices: Come up with a brand strategy and positioning that gets you in the top three (Visa versus American Express example) or create a new category ladder. I will explain more about category ladders in the next chapter.

Here is the key question you need to ask yourself about your brand: Which category ladder are you going to own in the mind of your prospect? You want to be the first brand someone thinks of on your category ladder. This is what leading brands do on purpose. Dominos was able to do it by being the first pizza delivery place that guaranteed pizza delivery in 30 minutes or less. Not better pizza, just pizza delivered hot and fresh in less than 30 minutes.

But if another company already owns the top rung of your category ladder, unless you are a strong number two, you should create a new ladder so that you can be first on that ladder. FedEx choose to create a category to be first in. And that category was overnight delivery. They came out with their marketing of "guaranteed when it absolutely positively has to be there

THE ART OF POSITIONING A BRAND.

overnight, it's Federal Express." They created the category of overnight delivery and they own that category in the customers mind. If you want something to be delivered overnight you think Federal Express because you know it's going to get there. That is the category that they chose to create and own. They took a ladder that was in somebody's mind about package delivery service and they actually created another ladder in that same category of *overnight delivery service* and they positioned themselves on the top rung of that *overnight delivery* ladder. That was decades ago and they still own that today. That is a great example of how you choose your ladder.

The same thing can happen to you with your brand. You can look at your brands marketplace and see where there might be a hole or a gap in that market. Even if there are four dozen other competitors in your market, there is an opportunity for you to position yourself as the expert in a category. Create an entirely new category ladder in the mind of the prospect and position yourself on the top rung of that ladder, just like Federal Express did with overnight delivery. Specifically focusing on their one message, and hammering it into our minds until we remembered FedEx without fail. And you can do the exact same thing. It's taking a category ladder and in a sense, dividing it down into a smaller and smaller niche, if you will. Do this well and you can own a category in the mind of your prospect. You just have to understand how the prospect thinks, what they need and how can you solve that problem or opportunity.

What did Apple do in 2007 when they were predominantly known as a computer company? They came out with a new ladder when they launched the iPhone. They're not really a phone company, they're a computer company. The "cellphone" ladder was already occupied. So Apple created (or at least refined) the "smartphone" ladder and made the iPhone the gold standard for smartphones. So now the iPhone is incredibly popular. Apple owns significant market share today because they understood how to do great branding and good marketing. Their marketers understood how to position the iPhone uniquely and differently so Apple was not fighting the same battle as most other companies. Even though Samsung is a formidable competitor, iPhones still cost more than Galaxy's. Arguably, all the other companies are still playing catch-up with Apple. Every category has a ladder in the mind of the prospect. You must think in terms of those categories, those ladders in the mind, because that's where the marketing battle is won or lost.

To create a new category ladder, you must position yourself for what you do and for what is unique about your brand. Then, focus your marketing on that. The customer is thinking specifically about their needs and about who can best solve their needs. They are looking for an expert or a leader. And when you have positioned yourself properly by choosing your ladder carefully, YOUR BRAND becomes that expert in their mind.

This has to be done methodically, and you have to be able to choose the ladder that relates to who you are and what your business is all about. That's exactly what Federal Express did. They chose a ladder, they chose the word "overnight," and they dominated that ladder. That's exactly what you can do in your brand marketing. It can be done. It's not that difficult. It just takes deep thinking and strategic planning and solid execution over a certain period of time. You need to look at your competition, know how the customer thinks, and make your choice carefully. There is always an opportunity for you to break out of the category mold and create your own category ladder. Your goal should be to own the top position on a ladder.

UNDERSTANDING BRAND POSITIONING

Brand positioning occurs whether or not a company is proactive in developing a position, however, if management takes an intelligent, forward-looking approach, it can positively influence its brand positioning in the eyes of its target customers. Otherwise the customer will position you and may not like it. Let's look at the concept of a brand positioning statement which is internal to the brand. Brand positioning statements are often confused with company taglines or slogans. Positioning statements are for internal use. These statements guide the marketing and operating decisions of your business. A positioning statement helps you make key decisions that affect your customer's perception of your brand. A tag line is an external statement used in your marketing efforts. Insights from your positioning statement can be turned into a tagline, but it is important to distinguish between the two.

The unfortunate reality is that no marketer has the power to position anything in the customer's mind, which is the core promise of positioning. The notion that positions are created by marketers has to die. Each customer has their own idea of what you are.

==Positioning is not something you do, but rather, is the result of your customer's perception of what you do.== Positioning is not something we can create in a vacuum; the act of positioning is a co-authored experience with the customers. Behind your positioning statement or tagline is your intention, how you desire your business or brand to be represented to customers. By examining the essence of what you are and comparing it with what your customers want, the doors open to building a business with a strong positioning in the mind of the customer. Why? Great brands merge their passion with their positioning into one statement that captures the essence of both.

PLACING YOUR BRAND POSITIONING IN YOUR CUSTOMER'S MIND

To position your brand in your customer's mind, you must start from within your business. Every member of your organization that "touches" or interacts with the customer has to be the perfect expression of your position. And, since everyone may come into contact with the customer in some way, every employee should be the best expression of your position. Now comes the hard part: Put up everything that represents your brand on a wall. List all your brand's touch points— every point of interac-tion with your customer. With a critical, yet intuitive eye, ask:

POSITIONING YOUR BRAND IN THE CONSUMER'S MIND

How can I more fluidly communicate my brand's desired position?

Does every touch point look, say, and feel like the brand I want my customers to perceive?

Many marketers don't have the clarity and conviction of following through on their words. Without certainty, you default to the status quo. Turn everything you do into an expression of your desired positioning and you can create something special. This takes courage; to actively position your brand means you have to stand for something. Only then are you truly on your way to owning your very own position in the minds of your customers.

BRAND POSITIONING STRATEGY PROCESS STEPS

In order to create a brand position strategy, you must first identify your brand's uniqueness and determine what differentiates you from your competition. This, by the way, takes a real critical view of your brand, product or service and lays it out on the table. If you have flaws or weaknesses with your brand, product or service, get them fixed or neutralized first. You can't do great brand work or marketing with a marginal product. Well, actually you could but you would just kill the product or worse, the company.

There are some key steps to effectively clarify your positioning in the marketplace:

- Determine how your brand is currently positioning itself
- Identify your direct competitors
- Understand how each competitor is positioning their brand
- Evaluate what is trending in your marketplace
- Compare your positioning to your competitors to identify your uniqueness
- Develop a distinct and value-based positioning idea
- Craft a brand positioning statement
- Test the efficacy of your brand positioning statement

CREATING YOUR BRAND POSITIONING STATEMENT

A positioning statement is an internal one or two sentence declaration that communicates your brand's unique value to your customers in relation to your main competitors. In the product technology book, Crossing the

Chasm, Geoffrey Moore offers one way of formulating a positioning statement:

> For **(target customer)** who **(statement of the need or opportunity)**, the **(product name)** is a **(product category)** that **(statement of key benefit;** also called a compelling reason to believe). Unlike **(primary competitive alternative)**, our product **(statement of primary differentiation)**.

However, I would like to provide a more simplified structure for formulating a brand positioning statement. There are four essential elements of a solid positioning statement:

> Target Customer: What is a concise summary of the attitudinal and demographic description of the target group of customers your brand is attempting to appeal to and attract?
>
> Market Definition: What category is your brand competing in and in what context does your brand have relevance to your customers?
>
> Brand Promise: What is the most compelling (emotional/rational) benefit to your target customers that your brand **can own** relative to your competition?
>
> Reason to Believe: What is the most compelling evidence that your brand can deliver on its brand promise?

After carefully research and thoughtfully answering these four questions, you can craft your "internal" brand positioning statement:

> For [target customers], [company name] is the [market definition] that delivers [brand promise] because only [company name] is [reason to believe].

To have you understand how to do this and what it looks like, here are two examples of positioning statements. Amazon.com used the following positioning statement in 2001 (when it almost exclusively sold books):

"For *World Wide Web users* who enjoy books, Amazon.com is *a online bookseller* that provides *instant access* to over 1.1 million books. Unlike traditional book retailers, Amazon.com provides a combination of *extraordinary convenience, low prices, and comprehensive selection.*"

Zipcar.com used the following positioning statement when it established its business in 2000:

"To *urban-dwelling, educated techno-savvy consumers,* when you use *Zipcar car-sharing service* instead of owning a car, *you save money* while *reducing your carbon footprint.*"

You can see how crafting an internal brand positioning statement really simplifies and clarifies exactly how you are different and to whom and why they should care. You need to do all of this carefully. And when you design your marketing campaign, hold the work up against this statement to see if you are still on strategy with your potential marketing messaging. Also, evaluate your brand positioning statement.

EVALUATE YOUR BRAND POSITIONING STATEMENT

Take your time and do your brand positioning statement well. An intelligent and well-crafted positioning statement is a powerful tool for bringing focus and clarity to your marketing strategies, advertising campaigns, and promotional tactics. If used properly, this statement can help you make effective decisions to help differentiate your brand, attract your target customers, and win market share from your competition. Here are several criteria for checking your brand positioning:

Does it differentiate your brand?

Does it match customer perceptions of your brand?

Does it enable company or brand growth?

Does it identify your brand's unique value to your customers?

Does it produce a clear picture in your mind that's different from your competitors?

Is it focused on your core customers?

Is it focused on new customers?

Is it memorable and motivating?

Is it consistent in all areas of your business?

Is it easy to understand?

Will it be difficult to copy by competitors?

Is it positioned for long-term success?

Is your brand promise believable and credible?

Can your brand uniquely own it?

Will it withstand counterattacks from your competitors?

Will it help you make more effective marketing and branding decisions?

Once you believe you have crafted a strong brand positioning statement, see if you can bring it alive with a powerful tagline.

THE USE OF TAGLINES IN BRAND POSITIONING

Now you know that brand positioning statements are internal to the company. Let's review how you bring that brand positioning statement alive in your marketing with the use of a tagline. Taglines are phrases that are written to convey not just the benefit of a product or service, but also to enhance the brand's personality. Why do you need a tagline? So people will quickly understand what you do and who you are. To ignite passion for your brand. And, if you're very lucky, to become part of the customer vernacular; remember "Where's the Beef?" for Wendy's? FedEx's tagline, "When it absolutely, positively has to be there overnight," set them up as a superior service and therefore a powerful brand. Miller Lite launched with a tagline that explained the product benefit: *Tastes Great. Less Filling*. Geico entices people with their tagline:

"*15 minutes can save you 15% or more on your car insurance.*" Campbell's was comfortable selling the soup category with the tagline, *Soup is Good Food*. Until the FDA challenged them because maybe, all that sodium wasn't

Nike	Just Do It.
BMW	The Ultimate Driving Machine.
Apple	Think Different.
McDonald's	I'm Lovin' It.

so good. They've reverted back to *Mmm! Mmm! Good!* Skittles 'call to action, *Taste the Rainbow*, definitely captures the fun spirit of the brand. Once you have a strong brand positioning statement you can create a tagline that helps establish the position you're looking to own.

Here are a few examples of key brands using a strong tagline line to support their brand position:

>Mercedes-Benz: The best or nothing.
>
>BMW: The ultimate driving machine.
>
>Southwest Airlines: Low fares.
>
>State Farm: Like a good neighbor, State Farm is there.
>
>Nike: Just do it.
>
>Coca-Cola: The real thing.
>
>Target: Expect more. Pay less.
>
>Volvo: For life.
>
>Home Depot: More saving, more doing.

You should not take your tagline lightly. It's not a flavor of the month marketing tactic. Do it well and it could catapult your brand to the top of that market category and be with you for years. Don't do it well and nothing will happen. Or worse, people will make fun of your tagline if it's not believable or just does not make sense. Dr. Pepper once used a tagline that was as follows, "*It's not for women*." Honestly, I don't get it at all. Why alienate all the women in the marketplace so you can appeal to some sort of macho place in teenage or adult male minds. What is the benefit? They ran it for a very short period of time and dropped it.

WHY BRAND POSITIONING IS CRITICAL

Brand positioning is a powerful strategy for setting your business up to thrive. It will help drive growth and build a business resilient enough to endure shifts in the market. So work to ensure it's designed to maximize the relevance of how and why your company matters to the people as it's important to sustaining growth and profitability. Markets, in their very nature, are dynamic, always shifting and progressing. Many businesses spend a lot of time, focus, and energy properly positioning their brand in the current market. And that alone, is hard to get right. But what many businesses fail to do is reassess their brand positioning down the road as needed. Markets change. Customers change. New competitors enter the industry. And companies develop and deploy new products, features, and benefits constantly. Note that maintaining your positioning doesn't necessarily ensure your brand will be relevant in the future. Your positioning needs to last in a dynamic environment. And if you need to shift your positioning, do it before your competition does.

Differentiation in today's overcrowded market-place is critical for growth and for businesses to cut through the clutter to survive. As a result, you must take the time to get it right. Focusing on brand positioning is the best way to ensure your business has a solid platform for sustained growth. And for your brand, focusing on positioning is the best way to find a meaningful space in the hearts and minds of the people vital to your success.

BRAND INSIGHT

This brand got its start as just a single small grocery store in Los Angles California. The founder did not want to compete with 7-11 stores or even large grocery stores. So he paid attention to trends and especially to the changing needs of customers. He noticed they were traveling more and often looked for food from other places of the world. But he did not want to create a "high end" store; he wanted a neighborhood type store that would offer regular people great products at a reasonable price. Well, what started as a single store with probably no marketing has evolved into Trader Joe's today. They reinforce their brand with their own products. Simple packaging with easy to read ingredients. A smaller store footprint with products people want. A light tropical and nautical theme. They don't do any marketing to speak of because they want to spend the savings on their employees and their products to the benefit of their customers. They have created a powerful brand that is rising right along with people who want to eat healthy and pay less for their food products. But not at the sacrifice of quality. Talk to people who shop at Trader Joe's and they will tell you that they "love" Trader Joe's. That is solid branding and great positioning in the customers' minds.

KEY TAKEAWAY

Most people would never believe that you could build a brand without marketing. Well, Starbucks never did any marketing in their early days. Neither did Google or Facebook. The key message here is to find a place in the customer's mind that you can own and then let them own it. Customers build the above brands, not marketing.

CHAPTER NINE
UNDERSTANDING MARKET CATEGORIES AND LADDERS.
* * *

While most marketers understand broad marketplaces, some do not understand that a large marketplace is made up of smaller market or "product" categories. Understanding this is critical when it comes to product development and then obviously to marketing. Let me give you an example. When I say bottled water, what do you think of? Do you think of Arrowhead Spring Water? SmartWater? Aquafina? Dasani? The reason it's important to understand how large markets can be made up of smaller product segments is to better understand possible opportunities. If I were a company or brand and told you I wanted to enter the $14 billion bottled water marketplace today, what would you say? That it is too large, too saturated, too competitive? But it continues to grow, soda sales continue to fall, the health trend continues to flourish. Your understanding of market categories within a marketplace is critical because if you look at marketing through this lens, then you might see opportunity to leverage a healthy consumer or perhaps changing tastes. You would see the opportunity to "marry" vitamins and water and create Vitamin Water.

In this chapter, I will explain and share thoughts and strategies on both market categories and consumer product ladders and why you need to own the top space on a ladder because consumers have too many choices.

CONSUMERS HAVE TOO MANY CHOICES

Once upon a time, there was just toothpaste. It was called Crest, or Colgate, or maybe Pepsodent. You chose your brand and went on your way. Today their brand offshoots and a myriad of competitors occupy entire shelves. Do you pick a product formulated to freshen breath, control tartar, whiten teeth, combat plaque, or attack gingivitis? Do you select another if you're older than 50, have sensitive teeth, sensitive gums, or sensitive enamel? And that's just the tip of the market category iceberg. I know, because those are just some of the 27 varieties of Crest being sold at a single store. Multiply your experience by other products on your shopping list, from mustard to shampoo, and you've turned a trip to the grocery store into a job requiring serious study. And the bewildering number of choices can obscure price disparities.

A new survey by the Consumer Reports National Research Center confirms that option overload can be a hindrance as well as help. Almost 80 percent of the 2,818 subscribers surveyed said they'd found an especially wide range of choices in the previous month, and 36 percent of those said they were overwhelmed by the information they had to process to make a buying decision. Between 1975 and 2008, the number of products in the average supermarket swelled from an average of 8,948 to almost 47,000, according to the Food Marketing Institute. In the past few years, that number has fallen slightly, in part because of a growth spurt among smaller stores. An abundance of choice can complicate decision-making, causing shoppers to freeze or postpone a purchase out of uncertainty and frustration. When they do make a choice, they're more likely to be dissatisfied because they think an un-chosen item might have been better. Five percent of respondents who found too many options said they had walked away empty-handed because the scope of choices made the selection too hard. More troubling is that when faced with an array of complex options, consumers tend to throw reason out the window and pick a product based on what's easiest to evaluate, not what's most important. That is why it is more important than ever to clearly understand what is going on in a broad marketplace, in a market category segment and to pay attention to changing consumer tastes based on trends. Customers simply have too many choices. Your goal as a marketer is to clearly be a leader in a market category and simplify the consumer decision-making process. If you don't do it, your competitor will.

ELIMINATE THE COMPETITION, CREATE A NEW CATEGORY

Many brands grapple with a fundamental problem: how do you profitably build revenues in hyper-competitive markets? Grabbing business from a competitor is a difficult and expensive proposition. Raising your prices, unless delicately handled, can be risky. Lowering your prices can just lead to a price war and reduce your gross margin. Driving incremental product innovation is a common strategy but one with low odds of success when the value-add may be minor and the product remains comparatively undifferentiated. There is a better approach to reigniting growth: create your own category.

Pursuing incremental innovation is a tough road to travel. Various estimates put the success rate of each new product or upgrade at only 10%-20%, resulting in wasted investment, unhappy customers and damaged marketing careers. However, there

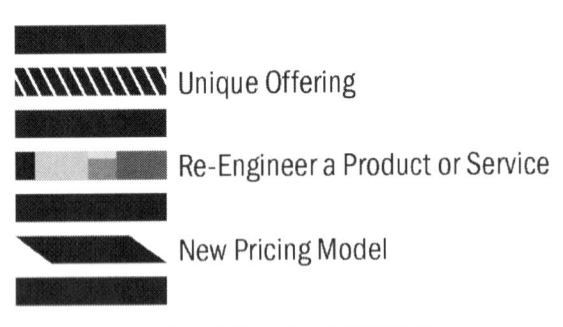

- Unique Offering
- Re-Engineer a Product or Service
- New Pricing Model

CREATE NEW MARKET CATEGORY

is a superior alternative for exploiting innovation. Create a new category. This proven product innovation approach combines cutting-edge product and business model innovation to create an entirely new offering, which by itself establishes a new category. There have been many successful examples of brands that have created new categories like Vitamin Water in bottled water marketplace, minivans by Chrysler, Greek-style yogurt by Chobani and the iTunes music store by Apple. According to research published in the Harvard Business Review, brands that create new categories generate much higher financial returns than incremental innovators. Specifically, 13 of the Fortune's 100 fastest-growing U.S. companies between

2009 and 2011 were considered category creators. They alone accounted for 53% of incremental revenue growth and 74% of incremental market capitalization growth of the top 100 over those three years

Category creators have to do a few things right to produce their industry-leading returns. First and foremost, they appeal to consumers by:

- Providing a unique offering that delivers compelling packaging, convenience, functionality or experiential benefits. Xbox, for example, enabled friends to play each other over the Internet.

- Creating a new pricing model that is attractive to consumers. For example, iTunes allowed consumers to buy only what they want (i.e. individual songs) at a low price.

- Re-engineering how a product is delivered and distributed. Consider how Netflix revolutionized the delivery of movies by leveraging internet-based, home delivery.

As a marketer, you have the ability to marshal resources and create powerful marketing campaigns. Before you do that, consider if it makes more sense to re-position or create a new category for your brand.

KEY ELEMENTS OF CATEGORY BUILDING

For a marketer, there are few professional experiences as exhilarating and inspiring as creating a new market category. There is no greater satisfaction than when customers tell you they cannot imagine doing their jobs without your product or that it has made their lives more enjoyable. Not to get too maudlin here, some products might not impact a customer's life that dramatically but it is still a marketing rush to change a marketplace. Beyond being personally rewarding, creating a new category is typically financially rewarding, too, with greater growth and higher valuations for the company or brand.

All this marketing glory comes with both challenges and frustrations, sometimes even in the same day. It's not an easy endeavor but with sound brand strategy, fortitude and perseverance you can make your vision of creating a new category a reality. Having helped create several categories in my marketing career, I've learned a few lessons that can be applied across all industries.

- Start with the why. Simon Sinek's book "*Start With the Why*" provides valuable insight on how great leaders inspire action. When it comes to creating a new category, it is all about the "why". People don't buy "what" you do or "how" you do it, they buy what they "feel" (even though product managers may beg to differ). It's difficult to create a category without inspiring others and getting them to realize they had a problem they didn't know existed or that fundamentally changes how they interact with the world. No one *asked* for Vitamin Water.

- Build the right team. Honestly, this sounds simple but I have seen other seemingly great marketing and product teams fail, not because of their talent, but because the team was not aligned correctly and did not have the buy in of top leadership. Another thing you need that's not easily examined is guts. It takes a certain amount of risk to succeed and some teams just can't seem to take the all-out risk. You also have to have a team that is not full of themselves and has a high degree of customer empathy. You can't create a team that just wants to "sell." They have to create the product or service with such a strong customer benefit in mind that the customer *wants* to buy.

- Bigger is not always better. Even with a huge marketing budget, it's tough to create a new category. However, it certainly can be done and doesn't always need to break the bank. In fact, a modest budget is often a driving force in being resourceful, creative and thinking about things differently. How do you find and leverage your most passionate enthusiasts? How do you make key influencers gush about you? How do you leverage social media to create unbridled demand for your product or service? When our team launched Amazon, we only focused on three key markets and targeted less than 1.4 million customers who we felt were critical influencers. We converted them and their word of mouth grew the online bookstore category.

- Competition is good. It may sound counterintuitive, but when you are creating a new category, competition helps legitimize a market and increases the size of the overall category pie. This is especially true for startups. You will actually benefit if others are spending their marketing dollars to help popularize the value of what you are doing. The key, however, is to preserve your first "mover" advantage, being first to market, and continue to find ways to elevate yourself above the crowd, while maintaining both a product and thought leader position. Never for one minute believe you don't have any competition. Perhaps nobody else in the market is doing exactly what you are doing, but your customers always have substitutes such as doing nothing or continuing with the status quo.

- Stay focused on your key marketing message. As tempting as it is when you have a team of passionate, creative people who want to jazz up your marketing messaging, success will be determined in the early days by consistently describing what you do and continuing to repeat the same message over and over and over until it clicks with your audience. Some companies focus on getting a product to market and then marketing it. But it is important to prime the market and spend significant time early on crafting your message, testing it in the market and then repeating it often. We launched Amazon and positioned them with the tagline "*Earth's Biggest Bookstore.*" We utilized simple strip ads that humorously highlighted the breadth of the Amazon book library and access to over a million titles. One example was, *"691 books on golf, 820 books on divorce. Amazon, Earth's Biggest Bookstore."* We showcased over 40 different book categories in that campaign for more than three years. I cannot tell how many times the creatives or the marketing team wanted to move to a new campaign I just said no.

Building a new market category is not for everyone. It takes vision, stamina and lots of guts. But when you get it right, there is amazing satisfaction for you, your company and the market that benefits from the new category created. Now that you better understand market categories let's turn to product ladders.

CONSUMER LADDERS: BASED ON BENEFITS

If you can simply grasp that consumers are in charge when it comes to purchasing a product or service, then as a marketer you have an advantage. Next, you need to understand that consumers organize or "categorize" almost all products or services into neat little ladders in their mind. Earlier in the book, I used the example of thinking of a car rental company and naming the top three brands that came into your mind. We can usually do three brands easily for each ladder: Enterprise, Hertz, Budget. Then for most people it kind of falls off rapidly. We can't as easily name the next three and so on. Most important, when you ask people to name the top three of any product or service, the order they give them to you is usually their own order of brand preference. So, if your brand is not in the top three, you are an also-ran.

One of the key things to understand about consumer product ladders is that consumers have a hierarchy of how they construct their ladder based on benefits. If you are even going to attempt to get onto the top rung on a consumer's ladder, understand and do the following:

- Define your target customers and understand their needs; listen to their "wants" but understand their needs. I want a Ferrari, but I need a cool car.

- Identify your unique brand feature, which is uniquely yours and what does it do that has a strong benefit to the customer?

- Deliver your message so that it is rationally understood by the customer; the consumer has to understand "what do I get?"

- If your product or service is powerful and unique to the customer, and they rationally understand the benefit, then they will hopefully move to a more emotional benefit of "feeling" positive. This is the holy grail of branding.

As marketers, it's important to understand how a potential customer thinks, rationalizes and then feels about a product or service. Because they will store the top brands on neat little ladders in their minds. And if you're not on the top rung or even on the ladder, you have a problem.

UNDERSTANDING THE RULES OF PRODUCT LADDERS

While being first in the mind of your customer should be your primary objective, the battle is not lost if you fail in this endeavor. All products are not created equal so there is a hierarchy in the mind that customers use in making decisions. For each category, there is a product ladder in the mind of the customer. On each rung is a brand name. The mind is selective and customers use the ladders in their mind in deciding which information to accept and which information to reject. In general, a mind accepts only new data that is consistent with the product ladder and where the brand is on the ladder ... *everything else is ignored.* As a marketer, you need to determine how many rungs there are on the product ladder in your potential customers mind and on which rung are you likely to be perceived. It depends on whether the product you are offering is a product used every day (like beverages, toothpaste, or cereal, referred to as high-interest products) or purchased infrequently (like travel packages, furniture, or wealth management) referred to as low-interest products.

If your product is a high-interest product, there are many rungs on the product ladder. If your product is low-interest product, there are fewer rungs on the ladder. And, there is a relationship between market share and your position on the ladder in your customer's mind. You tend to have twice the market share of the brand below you and half the market share of the brand above you. Sometimes your own ladder or category is too small. It might be better to be a small fish in a big pond than to be a big fish in a small pond. In other words, it is sometimes better to be number three on a big ladder than number one on a small ladder.

Let's look at how 7 Up used this law to its advantage by being a smaller fish in a bigger pond. On the lemon-lime soda ladder, 7 Up was on the top rung and Sprite was on the 2nd rung. However, in the beverage industry, the cola market is larger and therefore the ladder had more rungs. So 7 Up positioned itself in the mind of its customers with a marketing campaign called "The Uncola" and grabbed customers from the cola ladder and increased its sales.

Before you start any marketing program, you need to determine if your product is a high-interest or low-interest product; whether there are many or few rungs; and on which rung of the product ladder are you likely to be positioned in the mind of the customer. Then make sure your campaign deals realistically with your targeted position on the ladder. The marketing goal is to not emphasize why your product is better, feature and function-wise, over a competitor's but to develop a message that is recognized, accepted, and agreed to so that it will seduce and persuade a customer that what is offered will work for them. In other words, you are not selling toothpaste. You are selling white teeth.

Marketing done well is not a battle of products or services. It is all about the brand strategy and the positioning you use to have the consumer place your brand on their top product rung in their product or category ladder. Simple, right?

HOW DO YOU CREATE A NEW LADDER?

So, you are a marketer working with an agency or a company brand and you would like to create a new category or product ladder in your potential customer's mind. How do you do that? Well, you don't start with the notion that you have to come up with an innovative or breakthrough product. A better way to approach it is to examine the marketplace you are in or the marketplace you want to be in. I especially like large marketplaces as they have a high quantity of consumers who are familiar with the current product offerings. You don't have to waste time or money on educating people as to what yogurt is. They know. Create a perceptual map and place current brands in the grid based on elements important to the customer (e.g. quality vs. quantity, safety vs. cost, luxury vs. sporty and so on). Then look at your marketplace grid and look for noticeable gaps. Are these gaps large opportunities? Why have no other competitors moved into those gaps?

Next examine the industry you are in or might be targeting. Is it growing or in decline? Does it have relatively high competition or are there just a few players? What does it look like from a local, regional or global perspective? What do the research analysts say in their competitive analysis reports about the marketplace or the industry?

Last, look at the trends that might be impacting your current or potential customers. What are the key trends and how are they affecting large customer groups (e.g. Millennials, Baby Boomers, etc.) differently? Let's look a simple example of creating a new product ladder in the consumers mind based on an already large existing marketplace. Yogurt. In 2005, the yogurt marketplace in the USA was over $4 billion in revenue and dominated by three to four brands. Greek yogurt made up less than 4% of all yogurt sales. But times change and people are eating healthier. Millennials rise and want even better yogurt. Yogurt is impressively old: it dates back to the 3rd millennium B.C. But new brands arise and repackage and re-market Greek yogurt. Whether you believe it or not, what distinguishes Greek yogurt is its thicker, creamier texture because the liquid whey is strained out. Also, it contains probiotic cultures and is lower in lactose and has twice the protein content of regular yogurts. Remember, it's not what you believe, it's what consumers believe. And consumers, once introduced to Greek yogurt, wanted it. Today, the Greek yogurt market in the USA is over $3.5 billion and is forecasted to grow to over $4 billion by 2019. So, Greek yogurt alone will match 2005 USA yogurt sales ALL BT ITSELF BY 2019! And you thought the yogurt category was boring. In this case, the marketers created a new product ladder, Greek yogurt, in the consumer's mind out of an existing market category of yogurt. And new leaders on that product ladder like Chobani rose quickly to occupy the top rung on the ladder. It's been done time and time again in large markets. Enterprise Car Rental, Vitamin Water, Google, Neflix, Tesla, Starbucks, FaceBook, Amazon, etc. Look closely at the brands I just mentioned. Anyone of them create an entirely new market? No. They did something slightly or technologically different (but with an important customer benefit) and created a product ladder where they could occupy the top rung in the consumer's mind.

BRAND INSIGHT

This industry has motored along for over 100 years. Slow steady growth and relatively little innovation and disruption. Oh, there have been incremental improvements to the product over time but nothing radical. If you walked into the store in 2011 and saw these products in the aisle, you would not think twice. Yet this is a $13 billion industry. But two new companies arose in almost the same timeframe of 2011 to challenge the leaders in the industry. They both challenged the price and the business model. They had also accurately sensed that Millennials would support the disruption based on trends and patterns of this population. Both Harry's and Dollar Shave Club launched a new way to purchase razors, through an online subscription model. They challenged why anyone would willingly pay $4 to $15 for a razor after discovering how inexpensive is was to make razors. With little money for marketing, they utilized social media and created their own videos that poked fun at the industry leaders and asked target consumers to question why they were paying outrageous prices for razors. In less than five years, Dollar Shave Club grew so quickly that it was acquired for more than $1 billion.

KEY TAKEAWAY

It's not about the marketing. Clever marketing for these razor upstarts was not what led to their success. They successfully targeted a large market that had traditional high priced products and retail distribution. As marketers, look for opportunities to challenge the status quo in a way that aligns with the needs of a large population segment and shifting trends.

CHAPTER TEN
TRENDS AND BLUE OCEANS MATTER.
* * *

As a marketer, you have to understand your role and more importantly, your potential value. If you only understand how to get things done tactically, your value is diminished over time. If you learn the strategic "why" things have to be done, then clients or senior managers will value you for your knowledge and expertise and not just your capabilities. Early in my marketing career, I was a very tactical marketer; tell me what to do or what to get done and I got it done. Over time, and through years of mentoring and experience, I started to strategically advise clients what they had to do in order to be successful. In order to do this, I had to constantly stay abreast of trends and anticipate customer needs to the point where I had developed a five year market window "horizon" in my mind. That is, I felt, based on everything I could research, the knowledge of the marketplace, the competition, understanding customers and my marketing experience that I could tell a brand where it had to strategically go to grow or to survive in the next five years. That's when clients started hiring me and our agency for what we "knew" versus what we could do. Big difference.

So, take the time to learn your marketing craft and move toward becoming a brand expert. In this chapter, I will discuss emerging trends, two powerful customer groups and why blue oceans matter.

YOUR MARKETING LENS: FOCUSED ON TRENDS

Whether you believe it or not, if clients were to indicate why they hired you, either as a person or as a marketing agency, hopefully they would say it's for your ability to guide them as well as to get things done. If it's just to get things done, then you are a commodity. You need to provide more value and understand where things are going. As long as I can remember, I have always been focused on trends. Even trends that have no particular interest to me. But I knew that if I was going to be a brand and marketing expert, I had to be able to understand not just individual trends but how trends, customers, industries and timing might intersect. Because, sometimes in that intersection lays the real opportunity: Amazon. Even in the early days, it was the perfect intersection of technology, customers and an industry ripe for disruption. That's why Jeff Bezos trusted us to do the early branding and marketing for Amazon. Not because we were an integrated marketing agency and could do the work but because we did not think he was crazy; in fact, we thought it was the first really good idea and business model we had seen for the Internet since we saw the first webpage in late 1993. You need to understand your value as a marketer. Are you a commodity or moving toward being an expert?

spotting trends

CREATE A NEW CONSUMER LADDER

As a marketer, here are a few trends I think you should understand and keep an eye on:

- Mobile Internet: Increasingly inexpensive and capable mobile computing devices through cell and Internet connectivity

- Automation of knowledge work: Intelligent software systems that can perform knowledge work tasks involving unstructured commands and subtle judgments

- The Internet of Things: Networks of low-cost sensors and actuators for data collection, monitoring, decision making, and process optimization
- Cloud technology: Use of computer hardware and software resources delivered over a network or the Internet, often as a service
- Advanced robotics: Increasingly capable robots with enhanced senses, dexterity, and intelligence used to automate tasks or augment humans
- Autonomous and near-autonomous vehicles: Vehicles that can navigate and operate with reduced or no human intervention
- Next-generation genomics: Fast, low-cost gene sequencing, advanced big data analytics, and synthetic biology ("writing" DNA)
- Energy storage: Devices or systems that store energy for later use, including batteries
- AI or artificial intelligence: the capability of a machine to imitate intelligent human behavior
- 3D printing: Additive manufacturing techniques to create objects by printing layers of material based on digital models
- Advanced materials: Materials designed to have superior characteristics (e.g., strength, weight, conductivity) or functionality
- Renewable energy: Generation of electricity from renewable sources with reduced harmful climate impact
- Wearable devices: whether for health or fitness, Fitbits et al are here to stay
- Retail Subscription: Prime from Amazon, Birchbox and groceries delivered
- Organic/Natural Food: farm to table and everything in between
- Entertainment: Gaming and video content delivered through new mediums
- Pet Industry: dogs and cats have become our new best friends

- Rental Economy: Today, Uber and AirBnb, what will we rent next?
- AR/Virtual Reality: Watching sports and visiting islands, all from our living room

LEARNING TO SPOT TRENDS

There's nothing like being in the right place at the right time. Smart companies spend big money on research and development to ensure that their offerings are up to date — and to make sure they don't miss out on lucrative new opportunities. Traditionally, this practice has been the sole stomping ground of qualitative and quantitative research firms, but not anymore. After all, nobody anticipated that trendspotting itself would become a trend. Of course, forecasting and analyzing trends is not new. What is new is the emergence and widespread adoption of trendspotting by organizations as part of their innovation processes and as a way to anticipate what their customers will want in the future.

Why is this happening now? Many business leaders have lost confidence in traditional consumer research methodologies, especially when applied to innovation. Did Borders see Amazon coming? Why not? Why didn't Blockbuster react to the early emergence of Netflix? Why didn't Gillette see Dollar Shave Club? How did Nikon miss the "GoPro" social media trend? What's happening now is convergence of technology and the increasing acceleration of business and this is driving senior executive's quest for certainty and security in an unsure business world. The problem is they are so focused on their everyday business, they might not see a disruptive trend coming. That's where you come in. If you want to become a brand and marketing expert, you better be able to understand what is happening today and how that might impact tomorrow. Here are some tips to perhaps become a better trend spotter:

> *BECOME A BETTER READER.* Regularly read the leading publications and websites affecting your business. This could include industry publications, trade association sites, major newspapers, key business magazines, thought leaders and influential bloggers. So many trends start overseas (London, Paris, Tokyo) or on the coasts (Los

Angeles, Miami, San Francisco, New York), so make sure you read about what's going on in those cities. At first, scan information from a wide variety of sources -- from international news on down to niche bloggers focused on specific aspects of your industry. Obviously, there's a tsunami of information available. Use tech tools like RSS feeds, e-mail newsletters, Google Alerts or Twitter to keep on top of it all and get the info you want delivered to you when you want it. You'll quickly learn which sources are valuable and which you can jettison.

TALK TRENDS WITH PEOPLE. Talking to people is an equally important trend-spotting tactic. Start by getting involved in your industry's trade associations and attending events both online and offline. Network with other marketers, both in and out of your industry. (I promise, you'll gain some of your most valuable trend insights by talking to people in completely different industries.) Take advantage of social networking tools like LinkedIn and Facebook. Start or join groups on the networks and see what people are buzzing about. Pose questions about trends you're seeing and ask for feedback or comments. Also, watch your competition to see what they are doing.

WATCHING TRENDS. There's no substitute for getting out in the marketplace. Make it a point to regularly go where your target customers hang out. If your customers are teenagers, that might be the local mall. Well maybe not considering what's happening to malls right now...but even that is a trend. If they're businesspeople, it might be the region's "power lunch" restaurant or office park restaurant center. Spend some time simply watching and observing. What are people eating, doing, wearing, using? What stores or restaurants draw crowds and which sit empty? Trade shows are a great place to get trend ideas, too — even if you're not looking to buy anything it's worth attending many shows simply to see what's hot.

THINK ABOUT TRENDS. As you begin regularly gathering all this information, you'll start to develop a "trend-spotter mind." As you absorb and mull about what you've read, heard and observed, you'll start to make connections and observations that will lead to business-boosting insights. The news about rising interest in prepared food, the growth of free shipping and delivery services, the Millennial population which wants it now, spawns a new industry of food delivery to work or home.

Paraphrasing Steve Jobs, he once said in order to look forward you need to look backwards (perhaps the last ten years) and then connect the "future" dots. Well, be more curious and collect a lot of dots. Perhaps you can connect them and you'll be able to look forward. One thing you can definitely do that is fairly easy: be more curious. And pay special attention to two large population groups, Baby Boomers and Millennials.

MILLENNIALS AND BABY BOOMERS MATTER

It sounds trite but there has never been quite a time like the one we are in now. Baby Boomers have dominated our consumptive world for the past 50 years as a very large group of the population. I once thought, geez, could there ever be a bigger population than boomers who numbered 74.9 million in the USA in 2016? Ah, the answer would be yes. In 2016, Millennials passed boomers with 75.4 million and they are forecasted to grow to more than 80 million by 2025. In the United States, that will be three out of every four employees in the workplace. I don't care what you think about these two population groups. I don't pay attention to all the mindless chatter about "Millennial marketing" and why we should or should not focus on Millennials. The truth is it's not about what you think. This population group will dominate, disrupt, create and define the world we live in. Pay attention to them especially when they come into wealth as the baby boomers, who hold most of the wealth, continue to die off. Over the next 25 years, the biggest and wealthiest generation in U.S. history will transfer roughly **$30 trillion** in assets to their Gen X and millennial children. Let's look at these two groups a little closer.

Baby Boomers are going to represent an ongoing challenge to marketers not because of who they are but because of where they are going. They are not going to fade quietly into the sunset. Here are some facts and insights you need to understand if you are going to market to them.

- They have money. Baby Boomers currently spend upwards of 70% of the nation's disposable income. What's more is that they will inherit $13 trillion in the next 20 years.

- Real estate disruptors. The baby boomers created the suburbs and are not going to retire in retirement homes. They will live out their years in a place they call home and they will disrupt real estate as they get out of large homes into smaller ones especially in downtown locations.

- Brand loyal. They are very brand loyal and you better have a good reason for them to give up the brands they know and love. The good news is that if you can convert them to your brand, they will likely be very loyal.

- Fight the man. The Woodstock Music Festival was much more than a concert featuring the likes of Joan Baez, Janis Joplin, the Grateful Dead and Jimi Hendrix. It was a countercultural event which symbolized, among other things that the baby boomers were not going to be trussed up by their parent's morals and lifestyle. They would think and act for themselves – and they still want to be thought of that way. The least hint of patronizing the baby boomers will flatten any marketing campaign.

- They will not die. Okay, they will die eventually. If you think 'aged', 'senior' and 'elderly' are effective buzzwords for baby boomers – think again. They don't want to be reminded of their age, but of their accomplishments and of their future. I would advise marketers to concentrate on the 'bucket list' concept when pitching to baby boomers. They may have to buy adult diapers someday, but what they want to hear about is the best place to eat in Sturgis, South Dakota, when they ride their Harley Davidson there for the Rally in August.

- The bottom line is they have money to spend. They know they have earned the right to invest in themselves and their passions and hobbies and are ready to pay top dollar on travel, recreation and other leisure activities. As a marketer, you need to do your homework and know this group better. Your brand and/or clients will probably depend on it.

Let's move onto Millennials. They are a fascinating group to me. I actually like them. They are dreamers, have a social conscience, want it all now and are uncertain about their future. I actually think they will do a better job overall of running the world. If they could just get over their angst. ☺ As a marketer here are some insights and tips on how to market to millennials.

- Better be authentic. If you market a product or service to this crowd, you better be authentic. They will investigate back stories, read labels and listen to social media to determine your brand authenticity. Try to fool them and you are dead.

- They are social. Even the most novice marketer can spot the fact millennials are spending more time on social media than ever before. To reach this audience your brand has to be on social media with relevant conversations and content.

- Forget the hard sell. The hard sell has become something of a piece of satire in the eyes of millennials. They don't respond to the salesperson following them around screaming about how great their products are. The hard sell is gone and you need to let millennials make buying decisions for themselves. Don't believe me? Just watch a 25 year old Millennial walk into a traditional car dealership and walk out again in 20 minutes thinking salespeople are stupid. They know what they want to buy but no one was really listening.

- They move faster. The reason why millennials are moving fast is partly because of the mobile revolution. The rise of mobile has meant that they can stay connected wherever they happen to be. What it all means in practice is that marketing has turned into an omni-channel issue. Marketing strategies have to adapt to this. There's no such thing as online, offline, and mobile strategies. They've all been merged into one.

- Earn their loyalty. Millennials are not going to stick with the big name brands just because. The rise of millennials has forced brands to stop relying on the idea that they can "expect" to gain loyalty from customers. Marketers have to actively win and earn loyalty. This plays into the stereotype that millennials are disloyal and they won't stick with anything for any length of time. That demonstrates a fundamental misunderstanding. They may be harder to sway to your cause, but when they do become loyal they tend to be the most loyal consumers around.

So, what are the takeaways? Millennials represent significant buying power going forward, but they are not the only ones. Marketers would be well served to keep their eyes on both of these population groups. As a marketer, take the time and effort to understand the needs, actions, and buying patterns of both groups. Finally, marketing today needs to "speak" to consumers in a voice that is both authentic and genuine. If the message is stereotypical, both of these consumer groups have no reason to identify with a brand they feel does not accurately understand their needs or lifestyle. In terms of understanding consumers and marketplaces, heading for a blue ocean marketplace could be critical for your brand.

MARKETERS, SET SAIL FOR A BLUE OCEAN

For twenty years, I worked with big brands and startups as a marketing and branding expert and, with three other partners, built a $1 billion integrated marketing agency with more than 10,000 employees. Our job was to find out where our clients needed to go in the marketplace and provide them with the best opportunity for success. I have taught marketing and entrepreneurship courses at San Diego State University, and over the past few years, I have taught a course on Creativity and Innovation as part of the Entrepreneurship Program at the university. I wrote a book on creativity called *Simply Brilliant* so that I could teach students, and people worldwide, how to be more creative on purpose. One of the important concepts I teach students in my course is the notion of creating or heading for a "blue ocean" marketplace in an industry. This is something I did regularly as a brand and marketing expert. But I don't think most marketers today have heard of blue ocean strategy or even understand it at all. And yet, if you are a marketer and want to learn how to craft brands that change marketplaces, then how do you not know about blue ocean strategy? Ah, the Millennial digital marketer. ☺

I love using blue ocean strategy in the classroom. I loved using it in my professional marketing life. It's so simple to understand and it forces the students, and hopefully marketers today, to answer really simple questions regarding a current product or service:

> What can I eliminate?
>
> What can I reduce?
>
> What can I raise the bar on?
>
> What can I create that is new?

You can set sail for a blue ocean all in the hopes of creating a new product or service in a growing marketplace with little initial competition. Blue Ocean Strategy by Chan Kim and Renee Mauborgne was published in 2005 by Harvard Business School Press. It became a best-seller and still remains popular today. The authors' thesis is that most companies focus on competing against rivals for share in existing markets. Competition intensifies, features blossom, prices decline, and companies lose gross margin and profitability as competitors rush in to sell cheaper products in order to maintain market share. In this competitively intense ocean, segments are niched and products are commoditized turning the water red (either the red ink of losses or the blood of flailing competitors, choose your metaphor). So, if you find yourself competing on just price in either a growing or shrinking marketplace, the future is not bright.

The red ocean is simply where every mature industry is today. There is a defined market, defined competitors, and a typical business model in any specific industry. You initially compete on some differentiation and then slowly (or quickly in a rapidly growing marketplace) you start competing on some version of price or cost (e.g., AT&T versus Verizon, Samsung versus

LG, etc.). But you can choose to have a mindset that says you have to innovate in order to escape a red ocean and head to a blue ocean. How? Brands can choose to avoid this margin-eroding competitive intensity by putting less energy into red oceans and choosing instead to pioneer blue oceans—markets largely untapped by competition. By focusing beyond existing market demands, you can identify unmet needs (i.e., needs beyond lower price or incremental product improvements) and then innovate new solutions that create far more profitable uncontested markets—blue oceans.

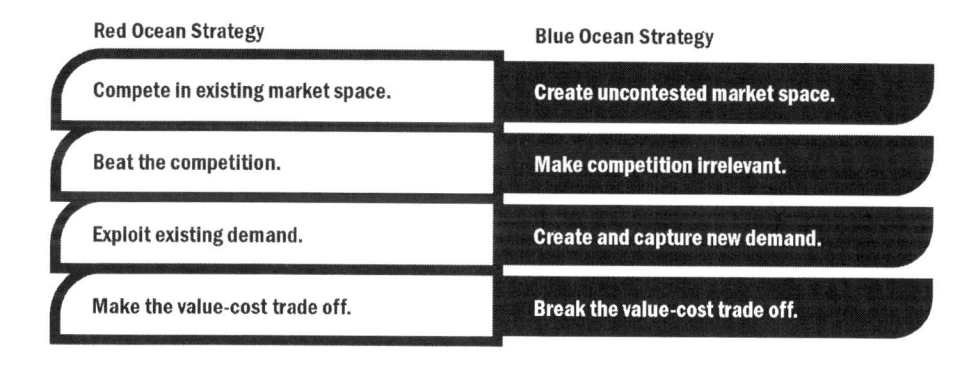

Red Ocean Strategy	Blue Ocean Strategy
Compete in existing market space.	Create uncontested market space.
Beat the competition.	Make competition irrelevant.
Exploit existing demand.	Create and capture new demand.
Make the value-cost trade off.	Break the value-cost trade off.

RED VS. BLUE OCEAN

Here are key elements of a marketing mindset regarding a blue ocean strategy perspective:

- Focus on current customers vs. focus on noncustomers. In most industries there is little effort to attract new buyers to the industry; the focus is on the customers currently purchasing in that industry. With a blue ocean mindset, there is a focus on trying to increase the size of the industry by attracting people who have never purchased in that industry. Think Apple with iTunes allowing everyone to buy digital music legally, online.

- Compete in existing markets vs. create uncontested markets to serve. Sounds good, right? But how do you do that? Existing markets are all the customers doing business in the industry right now, whether they are doing business with you or your competitors. If someone wins a customer, then it is assumed, someone will lose a customer. For someone to win, someone must lose. In uncontested markets, there is only a winner—you. No one else is fighting for the business because either they don't know about it or they don't know how. Think Cirque du Soleil in the early days attracting a more adult customer and a higher ticket price.

- Beat the competition vs. make the competition irrelevant. Competitors become irrelevant because they cannot duplicate the ideas in a way that is a commercial success. Remember, the whole idea of blue ocean strategy is to have high value at reasonable cost. If you are doing that, how can anyone compete with you? All the would-be competitors fall by the wayside. An example again is a company like Netflix, which rendered Blockbuster irrelevant due to Netflix's distribution model, first through the mail and then online.

- Exploit existing demand vs. create and capture new demand. You will be creating value so high that you will be attracting customers that never before would have considered entering the market. Nintendo's Wii appealed to families and seniors by raising the bar and creating a more interactive gaming experience. Yellow Tail wine attracted beer drinkers by eliminating the pretentious of wine and making it friendly. Southwest Airlines appealed to business travelers who spent days on the road by creating reduced flight costs for short trips. And the Apple iPad, a keyboard-free wireless tablet computer, gained appeal as a computing device for use by sales and service professionals and even as a next-generation, flat screen cash register.

BLUE OCEANS MATTER TO MARKETERS

Blue oceans matter because these markets are potentially large and with less competition, so there is more opportunity for you to grow as the dominant brand as long as you continue to innovate. What marketer, or brand, does not want a less competitive marketplace? Let's look at an example of a real company that created a blue ocean in their marketplace.

Netflix redefined the concept of "renting a movie." If you were a marketer and you met with Reed Hastings in 1997 and he told you what he thought they were going to build, what marketing advice would you have given him? "Ah, you are going up against Blockbuster, don't waste your time." "People are not going to watch movies online." If you want to create a blue ocean in an emerging marketplace, you have to get there slightly before everyone else does. Yes, it's a bit of risk and timing is everything but if you do it right, that marketplace is yours. Let's look at the elements of blue ocean strategy and better understand what Netflix did.

Which of the factors that the industry takes for granted should be eliminated? In the case of Netflix, they eliminated the stores.

Which factors should be reduced well below the industry's standard? Netflix had no late fees.

Which factors should be raised well above the industry's standard? Netflix let you rent three movies of your choice at one time with no due date. Simply return those at some point and then you could rent three more.

Which factors should be created that the industry has never offered? Netflix put their entire catalog online, you paid your monthly fee on a subscription basis and it was a flat monthly fee, not based on the individual movie.

Well, let's review how their blue ocean strategy worked out. Blockbuster, in 2004 had revenue of almost $6 billion. They went into final bankruptcy in 2013. Netflix at the end of 2016, had $8.8 billion in revenue.

MARKETERS, AVOID FIVE RED OCEAN TRAPS

As marketers you need to understand the marketplace where your company or brand exists and determine if it's in a red ocean. If it is in a red ocean, and you plan to aim for a blue ocean, avoid these five red ocean traps:

Focus on existing customers. This strategy will never lead you to expand your market or move away from your red ocean. Making your current customers happier in a red ocean, long-term, will just lead to even more competition. It is better to focus on non-customers and grow the segment and marketplace. If you owned a taxi company and tried to make current customers happier, you would never create Uber.

Focus on niche markets. While this may get you to a leadership position of a niche market, unless you have the opportunity to combine or attract additional segments of customers, you are still in a niche. Tesla, if it's going to grow, needs to move down from luxury (only 10% of the automotive marketplace) and attract bigger customer segments with quality and a lower price.

Innovation alone is not enough. While innovation is awesome for differentiation, it is not enough. Quicken did not just move accounting into the cloud with QuickBooks, but they did it with quality and a lower price. It's not the Uber app that allowed Uber to grow so quickly. And while Starbucks has utilized technology in several ways in its business, all three examples here also demonstrated "value" to the customer. Innovation without value is a problem.

Market creation does not have to be destructive. You don't have to disrupt a marketplace and take down current companies. You can move into a marketplace with "creative" disruption" and actually grow the marketplace without intentionally eliminating anyone. Viagra is a great example. Nintendo's Wii is another, attracting children and families to play games.

You don't have to be the low price leader. You don't necessarily need to move into or create a new market exclusively with a low price strategy. Instead it can be created at the high end, as Cirque du Soleil did in the circus industry, iPhone did in smart phones and Dyson did in vacuum cleaners. Even when companies do successfully create new markets at the low end, their offerings also are clearly differentiated. Salesforce.com, for instance, stands out for its ease of use, flexible subscription terms, hassle-free maintenance and ubiquitous access, while IKEA appeals to millions of people around the world with its standardized, stylish and easy to assemble furniture. Both are differentiated and low cost but with strong value to the customer.

While trends and blue oceans are important to marketers, it's also important to understand that marketing in general has changed. In the next chapter I will share with you how the 4 P's (product, price, place, promotion) have changed and what you need to know in order to be an effective marketer.

BRAND INSIGHT

This well-known brand is a goliath in the retail marketplace. In 2016, they had more than $485 billion in sales. They are huge. And they might be in trouble. From a branding perspective, in spite of their size, their brand is weak for several reasons. They are primarily positioned on low price, never a good thing, and they are known for a lousy shopping experience, poor customer service, and disorganized stores to many customers. Many people, from a branding perspective, in the USA see them as cheap, substandard and boring. A few years ago, jumping on a discount fad in the recession, they opened over 100 smaller stores competing in the "dollar store" marketplace. Those stores failed. For a company of this gargantuan size, Walmart is in trouble. Amazon has been relentless in matching their pricing but delivering more value. Costco is becoming more aggressive. Target is opening small "city-based" stores in urban environments. A major problem with Walmart is that their brand is perceived so weakly. That means they have to compete, ultimately, on customer service. It will be interesting to see whether or not they evolve.

KEY TAKEAWAY

No matter your size, you better have a strong brand. And you better focus on building value with your current and potential customers. If you have to build or defend your brand on price or customer service, then your customer service better be amazing. If it's not, you are left with the brand differentiation of price. The competition will match that, leaving you with nothing.

CHAPTER ELEVEN
4 P'S OF MARKETING HAVE CHANGED.
* * *

Early on in my 20 year marketing career, I was rather naïve about marketing. I did not really know how the art and science of how marketing came together to create and enable sales. I thought, rather simply, people made things and other people bought those things. As I started to understand and learn marketing, I could see that marketing was a very sophisticated "dance" between brands and consumers. And while most marketers don't influence the creation of the product, we certainly could impact the other three P's of price, place and promotion. I focused mostly on place and promotion in the early days as distribution channels were well defined and quite a few times, what separated similar products were the special promotions we created. Looking back, it was all rather well defined. Not so much today.

As a marketing professional, you're likely familiar with the 4 P's of the marketing mix: product, price, place and promotion. Whether you first discovered these industry pillars as an eager marketing major or uncovered them later on as you pursued your professional career, you needed to understand how they contributed to a comprehensive marketing strategy. What you may not know is that the 4 P's have changed. Why? I will review what has changed and what you need to consider today but first, let's take a look at the history of how the 4 P's were developed and accepted.

A HISTORY PERSPECTIVE OF THE 4 P'S

The origins of the 4 P's" can be traced to the late 1940s. The first known mention of a marketing mix has been attributed to a Professor of Marketing at Harvard University, Prof. James Culliton. In 1948, Culliton published an article entitled, The Management of Marketing Costs in which Culliton describes marketers as "mixers of ingredients". Some years later, Culliton's colleague, Professor Neil Borden, published a retrospective article detailing the early history of the marketing mix in which he claims that he was inspired by Culliton's idea of "mixer", and credits him with popularizing the concept of the "marketing mix". According to Borden's account, he used the term, "marketing mix" consistently from the late 1940s. For instance, he is known to have used the term marketing mix in his presidential address given to the American Marketing Association in 1953. Borden states, "When building a marketing program to fit the needs of his firm, the marketing manager has to weigh the behavioral forces and then juggle marketing elements in his mix with a keen eye on the resources with which he has to work."

Although the idea of marketers as mixers of ingredients caught on, marketers could not reach any real consensus about what elements should be included in the mix until the 1960s. The 4 P's, in its modern form, was first proposed in 1960 by E. Jerome McCarthy in his text-book, Basic Marketing: A Managerial Approach. McCarthy used the 4 P's as an organizing framework with chapters devoted to each of the elements, contained within a managerial approach that also included chapters dedicated to analysis, consumer behavior, marketing research, market segmentation and planning to round out the managerial approach. According to McCarthy the marketers essentially have these four variables which they can use while crafting a marketing strategy and writing a marketing plan. In the long term, all four of the mix variables can be changed, but in the short term it is difficult to modify the product or the distribution channel. Phillip Kotler, a prolific author, popularized the managerial approach, and with it, spread the concept of the 4 P's. McCarthy's 4 P's have been widely adopted by both marketing academics and practitioners.

THE DEFINITION OF THE 4 P'S

In order to better understand what has changed regarding the 4 P's, let's look at their simple definition:

- **Product** refers to what the business offers for sale, which may include products or services. Product decisions include the quality, features, benefits, style, design, branding, packaging, services, warranties, guarantees, life cycles, investments and returns.

    Product
    Price
    Place
    Promotion

- **Price** refers to decisions surrounding list pricing, discount pricing, special offer pricing, credit payment or credit terms. Price refers to the total cost to customer to acquire the product, and may involve both monetary and psychological costs such as the time and effort expended in acquisition.

- **Place** is defined as the direct or indirect channels to market, geographical distribution, territorial coverage, retail outlet, market location, catalogues, inventory, logistics and order fulfilment. Place refers either to the physical location where a business carries out business or the distribution channels used to reach markets. Place may refer to a retail outlet, but increasingly refers to virtual stores such as a telephone call center or an ecommerce website.

- **Promotion** refers to the marketing communication used to make the offer known to potential customers and persuade them to investigate it further. Promotion elements include advertising, public relations, direct selling, online marketing and sales promotions.

While it's certainly easy to understand the definitions of the 4 P's, what is not so easy to understand is how much they have changed. Why? Well, two major things have occurred.

THIS LITTLE THING CALLED THE INTERNET

If you think about the 4 P's (place, price, product, promotion) it seems like they are ordered principles. Well, the Internet changed all of that forever. It's not just that the Internet is a new technology or a new distribution channel; it's more powerful than that. With dynamic software and powerful ecommerce engines, you can now offer dynamic pricing, customize the product offering, vary the promotion and often times and modify the place the product is delivered. You order that pizza special? You want that pizza to go? You want it delivered? The Internet has unleashed such variability and freedom to specialize and customize the product offering. Combine that with the rise of smartphones and the powerful mobility that it brings; all using apps connected to some "front end" brand that is connected to a powerful database "back-end" and the opportunity to serve the customer is endless.

At the same time, the Internet has flattened competitive playing fields. If you wanted to participate in certain marketplaces in the past, you needed a large investment, lots of employees and large marketing budgets. Not anymore. You want to open a subscription organic dog food business that competes with Petco? No problem. Just build a website using open source tools, design a good brand, outsource the creation and delivery of the dog food to the manufacturing company and run the whole thing from your condo. The power of the technology today to remove substantial costs from operating a business is staggering. And if you are adept at understanding simple, powerful branding and know how to leverage social media marketing, then you can create and launch the beginnings of a company with very little investment or perhaps even risk. So, if technology is having this massive impact on marketing, what else has changed?

MILLENNIALS ARE CHANGING THE GAME

I know it's an often used term: "There has never been a time like this before." And perhaps even the Romans used that phrase. But if you look at the rise of the Millennial population, weaned on iPads and smartphones, surrounded by "just now" media options and cuddled on their bed watching their favorite shows via their laptop, this generation of 81 million by 2025 are leading massive changes. They are a smart generation but are not great at face-to-face communication. They don't have as much patience to get what they want, but they will be kinder to social causes. They will be more educated not as a pursuit but as a requirement. They are extremely technology savvy and love shopping online. They are single-handedly crushing retail businesses. Not because they want to. But because they are efficient and a bit lazy. They value what they do with their time. Even if they are doing nothing! They would rather order five pieces of clothing from an online store, try them on at home, and then send back the four items they don't like rather than going to the mall. Why? It just takes too much time and energy to go to the mall. And you might have to talk to store clerks. Don't want to. I am not saying it's a good thing that traditional malls are dying. But I don't think it's a bad thing either. Maybe real estate developers can take today's malls and build more affordable housing and living spaces.

If you are going to create marketing strategies and campaigns, you need to understand the changes and more importantly understand that the 4 P's have changed forever.

THE RE-INVENTION OF THE 4 P'S

Marketers today need to understand that the power and control of marketing has shifted to the customer. The customer, through all the online research, social media, product reviews and word of mouth, knows quite a bit of information about your product and service. And potentially, they are already forming brand impressions way before you ever engage them. Today's customers are looking for adaptable products that meet their specific needs in an innovative way. Remember that innovation means providing something new that customers actually want. And new doesn't always mean whiz-bang technology; it can simply be a basic product at a basic price. Dollar Shave Club

So if you believe the customer has more information and control and that the original 4 P's of marketing have to evolve, then what comes next?

THE NEW 4 P'S OF MARKETING

Rather than get hung up in the taxonomy of the 4 P's, remember it's just a term to identify the marketing mix. Assume things have changed and you need a new point of view on the marketing mix in order to better engage and sell to customers. Here is what I believe you need to focus on as you build your brand strategy and marketing campaigns.

- **Solution instead of Product.** Customers don't care about product features or usability if a product fails to *solve* their problem. Having a quality product today is just the entry price to be in the market. It's not about the features you want your product to have, it's about the problems that customers need to solve. Solve their problem better than anyone else and you'll end up with a product your customers can't live without.

    Solution
    Accessibility
    Value
    Education

    Too often, businesses get caught up in the features, functions and technological superiority of their product over the competition. The reality is that none of that matters to customers if they can't clearly match the outcomes being promised to the problems they have. If you're building a product or service based on features and not based on customer needs, you're working backwards.

- **Accessibility instead of Place.** In an age where many businesses operate around always-on, high speed Internet access, "place" is irrelevant to the customer. When you can dip into almost the entirety of the world's knowledge from the phone in your pocket, you're always able to research, buy and advocate. It's not about Place any longer. Now, it's about Accessibility. What can a brand give me at this precise moment that I want or need? That's the "bar" companies now have to clear, and it's not going to be easy. Customers want your products and business to be accessible almost anywhere and anytime and not just for the product purchase. They want to know that your support will have their backs. To achieve this, they need to see you engaging with other customers to get a sense that you'll be there should something go wrong.

- **Value instead of Price**. If customers occasionally tell you that your product is too expensive, what they might really be saying is that your product does not deliver enough value for that price. When you hear customers say that your product is too expensive, before lowering the price, become obsessed with how to increase the product's value. That orientation is vital in directing the drive toward improving a product without competing against others on a downward spiral based on price. No brand, long-term, wins on price. While customers may have concerns about price, that comes after their concerns about value. Clear, compelling communication about the benefits of your product is how you gain pricing power.

- **Education and Information instead of Promotion.** Marketers today need to shift from simple promotional displays and messages and provide more educational content and engagement. Customers today are getting used to doing some product or service research, rationalization and comparison, so help educate and inform them. Why is this important? Simply providing your potential customers with free, valuable and useful information creates a much stronger bond and connection than any banner ad or press mention ever could. The old methods of marketing were focused on interruption, but the marketer of today has the opportunity to be involved with customers' needs at each point in the evaluation and purchase cycle. In many ways today, businesses can act as "education" surrogates, providing current and potential customers with information and advice that helps them do their job better or make their lives easier. This creates a sense of familiarity and trust long before a purchase is even made.

The creation, intent and delivery of the 4 P's of marketing have to change in the face of all that has changed in the last 20 years with regard to technology, disruptive channels and the well informed customer. Marketers today need to accept that the customer has more control in the marketing mix than ever before. So, accept and leverage that and give the customer what they want. Just make sure you do it in a way that differentiates your brand or you will be competing on price. All the way to the bottom.

BRAND INSIGHT

It pays to listen as a brand and evolve to the changing needs of your customers. This brand started as a 10-person company making wooden toys in 1939. A quiet almost sleepy little company, it meandered along for years. Its original breakthrough moved it into the world of "plastics" and it focused almost all of its energy on marketing to children. But along their journey, they noticed that a major part of its target audience, who were once their customers as children, were now engaging with their products. So they shifted their marketing attention to adults and begin to create massively sophisticated versions of their new "toys." That led to another revelation and the brand decided to create physical spaces where all of its customers could venture inside of an almost customer created world. Top that off with an almost ridiculous idea, to create a movie featuring the toys which was unbelievably successful with over $400 million in movie revenue. Lego has listened and adapted well. For almost anyone who has played with Lego's, gone to LegoLand or watched the Lego movie, when you say the word "lego" it usually brings a smile to someone's face. Lego is still a very powerful and relevant brand. I can't even think of a competitor.

KEY TAKEAWAY

As you work with your brand or a client's brand, listen intensely to the customer and continuously monitor the marketplace. Think of ways to evolve and engage your customers that is not necessarily product focused but more "value" driven. Think of ways your brand can *delight* your customers. That should spark new product or service ideas that your brand has the permission to bring to the marketplace.

CHAPTER TWELVE

BUILD A BRAND: THE POWER OF INTEGRATED MARKETING.
* * *

As a digital marketer, hopefully, you are beginning to understand the power of good branding, to create that "internal" feeling within your customer and then use the "external" marketing campaign to drive your communication messages. Regardless of media channels used, your branding and marketing need to seamlessly mesh using the same images, voice, creative design and messages to drive home your brand positioning. So, if you design a brand identity for your client or brand, build a website, create online communication assets (e.g. online ads, videos, tweet, blog posts, etc.) it all works together with the same common "look and feel." You may not know exactly where your customer "hears or sees" your communication and they may only get a piece here and there. That's why the synergy of integrated marketing communications is so powerful. But it wasn't always this way.

INTEGRATED MARKETING IS BORN

If you Google the words "integrated marketing communications" you will find university research mentions that integrated marketing as a research concept started around 1993. Not true. CKS|Partners was created in 1991. Our agency was born from the principles of five marketers who all believed that marketing in the late 80's and early 90's was changing forever. Or more importantly, customers were changing. Previously, advertising in all forms dominated marketing. In 1989, the CEO of a leading advertising agency in New York was asked about the possible "dis-intermediation" of media, and he replied, "Traditional advertising has and will rule the marketing landscape for a very long time." I was in New York at the time doing marketing work for Mercedes Benz and when I heard those words, they rang hollow. In the late 80's I was watching little cracks appear in the stranglehold that traditional advertising had in the marketing world. I watched music CD's arrive and thought, wow if we can put "digital" music on CD's what else can we do? Can we create CD/DVD multimedia animations? Can we create interactive product demonstrations? Outdoor media was growing, direct mail and sales promotions were growing. Large events started to grow led by key product sponsors. Casinos in Las Vegas were using digital displays to promote shows. Cable TV was exploding and that meant we no longer had just three to four major television channels, we had 500 or more on this new thing called cable. I went to communication and technology trade shows and saw companies like Philips demonstrate interactive DVD players that they would be bringing to the market in a few years. There were major customer shifts occurring as well. We were moving faster from an industrial world to a world of knowledge workers and service employment. Education levels were rising and people were getting smarter. In a marketing sense, people no longer believed everything they saw on television. With all these new forms of emerging media bringing information, the customers had more information and therefore, more choice.

I could "feel" the marketing landscape changing and knew the marketers in New York were clueless about the coming changes, so I went to where I thought the edge of marketing in the USA might be and that was California. Specifically, Silicon Valley. I moved to San Francisco to work with Apple on some of their marketing initiatives but I really moved to find the other two to three people like me that could see marketing was going to change and together we would create a new kind of marketing agency around integrated marketing. Within six months of working at Apple, I found them. A small design boutique founded by three of the brightest marketing people I had ever met. Over the next year, we had multiple conversations about the future of marketing and I joined them at the end of that year. We focused on designing integrated marketing communications for the brands we worked with and offered no advertising media services. Traditional advertising agencies in Silicon Valley and San Francisco literally laughed at us. By the way, if you are going to be a leader, most people won't get where you are going as you will be moving against the crowd. It takes a certain amount of risk to be a leader. We started with little companies like Adobe, McAfee, and two Steve Jobs companies, NEXT and Pixar. Other brands that needed to move faster noticed our great integrated marketing work came next and we moved up to United Airlines, Levi's and Amazon. Now we were a brand expert whose expertise was founded in integrated marketing. While we only wanted to create the best integrated marketing communications agency in the world, we went on to create the largest with over 10,000 employees, 65 offices in 30 countries and $1.2 billion in revenue. In hindsight, we should have only created the best agency as we lost control of the company through our IPO (initial public offering) and subsequent mergers. In 2001, the entire company went away through bankruptcy. Honestly, it was arguably the best years of our "marketing" lives as we solidified the notion that brands would have to be centered on an integrated marketing approach. We were the first agency to do work with and for "digital" brands like Yahoo!, Amazon, eBay and for about seven years, we were on the edge of everything that mattered in marketing.

Enough nostalgia. Let's delve into integrated marketing and have you understand why it's even more critical today than ever before to have a brand be supported by an integrated marketing strategy.

WHY INTEGRATED MARKETING IS NECESSARY

Today, the world is moving faster and competitors can seemingly come out of nowhere. It's not enough for companies to create amazing products and services; brands must communicate the value and benefits of the offerings to both current and potential customers in both business-to-business and business-to-consumer markets. Integrated marketing communications (IMC) provides an approach designed to *deliver one consistent message* to buyers across a brand's marketing communication mediums that may span all different types of media—TV, radio, magazines, the Internet, outdoor, mobile phones, and so forth. For example, Campbell's

Soup company typically includes the "Mm, mm good" slogan in the print ads it places in newspapers and magazines, in ads on the Internet, and in commercials on television and radio. A company's communications should support a consistent message even if it is trying to reach different audiences. You might "say it" in different ways but the same message should still come through.

Integrated Marketing Campaign: Website, Social Media, Public Relations, Search Marketing & SEO, Events, Advertising, Direct Marketing, Email Marketing, Internal Communications, TV/Radio

Changes in communication technology and instant access to information through tools such as the Internet explain one of the reasons why integrated marketing communication has become so important. Delivering consistent information about a brand or a product helps establish the brand in the minds of consumers and potential customers. Many consumers and business professionals seek information and connect with other people and businesses from their computers and phones. The work and social environments are changing, with more people having virtual offices and texting on their cell phones or communicating through social media such as Facebook. Text messaging, Internet, smartphones, blogs—the way we communicate continues to change the way companies are doing business and reaching their customers. As a result, organizations have realized they need to change their marketing strategies as well to reach specific audiences.

Traditional media (magazines, newspapers, television) is on the decline and now compete with media such as the Internet, texting, and mobile phones; user-generated content such as blogs, reviews and YouTube; and out-of-home advertising such as billboards and movable car-based promotion platforms like Wrapify. As the media landscape continues to change, marketers may change the type of marketing communications they use in order to reach their target markets via a specific media channel. Regardless of the type of media used, marketers should use an integrated marketing communications approach to deliver one consistent message to buyers. It's really the only way to build and support a brand today. Here are a few reasons why you need to embrace an integrated marketing communications approach for your brand:

> The sheer volume of existing communication channels combined with the rapid introduction of new channels and technologies.
>
> The vast differences in customer behavior, expectations and types of business interactions within each channel.
>
> The extremely fast pace at which content is shared and the very short lifespan (sometimes mere minutes) of that content.
>
> The somewhat uncomfortable fact that customers now share control of the conversation.
>
> The ever-increasing growth of mobile and the resulting need to integrate online and place-based experiences.
>
> The strong customer demand for access and convenience.

Your brand needs to work harder than ever before. If you don't leverage the synergy of integrated marketing communications, you risk confusing your customer and not creating a powerful brand in their minds. More than ever customers are in control. Let them find you via their channel of choice. Just be there with a consistent look, feel and message to support your brand. Let me remind you of the difference between branding and integrated marketing.

BRANDING AND INTEGRATED MARKETING

A brand is made up of far more than a name and a logo. A 'brand' is the holistic perception and recognition, whether positive or negative, of an entity that makes it stand out from its competition. Building a brand is no small task, yet it plays a substantial role in developing a company's reputation and value. But to build a successful brand, marketer's first need to know exactly what branding is. The terms 'branding' and 'marketing' are frequently confused with each other, even by professionals. While branding can be described as the expression of value of an entity, marketing refers to the process of promoting an entity's products and services (or the entity itself). Strong marketing will result in the development of brand value. However, simply promoting products and services through marketing channels without applying a branding system can create a confused overall brand message, resulting in reduced efficiency, and reduced effect. This is where integrated marketing communications comes in.

IMC is crucial today due to the fragmentation of the media market. Previously, consumers received advertising from brands through mass media outlets such as TV, print or radio. The communication model was called "push" and the messages were "one to many", with the company retaining control of the messaging. In the current digital landscape, audiences are spread out thinly across multiple media channels. This has changed the dynamic to one where communication is interactive, and consumers are more active multi-taskers and are increasingly interconnected and "ubiquitous." As a result, consumers are engaging with brands at new touch points and have a co-creating role in brand identity. Brands that do IMC poorly present a divided and fractured voice to the consumer.

Let's better define the components of integrated marketing. Integrated marketing communications (IMC) "is the organization, planning, and monitoring of marketing components and data to control and influence brand information, associations, and experiences" (Hosford-Dunn, 2006). In other words, IMC is essentially the bridge between marketing and branding.

With advances in digital platforms, there is a growing number of ways in which a company can communicate with a consumer. If you look at the integrated marketing communications chart, you can see all the different forms of marketing and I have left quite a few others off this chart. IMC brings together all the communication content that is possible to be transmitted via all available communication channels – including advertising, promotions, online, events and sponsorships – to deliver a unified message to potential and existing customers. Your company's brand therefore emerges from the sum of all points of contact that the consumer has with your company. From a consumer's perspective, "hearing and seeing" the same message from the company through every media channel, from social media to television and print, increases the brand's integrity and helps to establish it in the consumer's mind. The consumer then becomes more likely to feel an attachment, or a level of trust, for the brand. That in turn creates the customer "feeling" that there is no substitute for your brand. Integrated communications should develop and maintain a healthy two-way relationship with the consumer. This is particularly important for maintaining brand value, since today's consumers expect to be able to interact with brands before, during and after a purchase or service. In other words, "IMC builds the relationships that builds brands". IMC is customer-centric – meaning that it focuses on meeting the requirements of the target market by taking into account customer feedback.

Let's put all this in perspective for a digital marketer today. Imagine you land a company that has a consumer food product. They are about $25 million in sales and have several products sold through specialty stores and online. Obviously there is product packaging, brand and marketing work that has been done before you arrived. They hired you or your agency to do better work online either to build brand awareness or drive online sales. Before you do anything, you better understand everything they are currently doing and understand the brand. Ask these questions:

> What's the story of your brand or company?

> What does your brand stand for in your customers' minds?

How is the brand positioned?

What total marketing have you done to date?

What does the product packaging look like?

What are the key product marketing messages?

Who are your competitors?

They may be hiring you for your digital marketing expertise initially, but if you show the brand that you understand branding, they will see you in a more strategic light and possibly give you other responsibilities or marketing campaigns. You have to know the whole picture of the brand or marketing strategy even if you are only doing SEO, content, analytics and an AdWords campaign. What you create or write has to match the brand "voice" and contribute to the look and feel of the brand. The benefits of doing this are powerful.

THE BENEFITS OF IMC

It's not just me or my point of view regarding integrated marketing communications. The research now validates the power and synergy of an integrated marketing communications strategy. An IMC approach provides benefits at every level of the company including:

> Operational level – reduces transaction costs, interdepartmental conflict, and duplication of effort
>
> Campaign level – creates synergy with the marketing communications mix and provides a higher return on campaign investment vs. the competition
>
> Brand level – provides clarity and consistency to the brand messages to create brand loyal customers
>
> Customer level – positively impacts consumer awareness, customer attitudes, and customer experiences at every touch point

Market level – decreases the rate of defection, increases market position and loyalty, sales, and sales growth

Financial level – increases the ability to achieve higher sales, sales growth, profitability, return on investment (ROI), and return on brand investment (ROBI) vs. the competition

As a marketer, you need to understand the difference between branding and marketing and then employ an integrated marketing communications "mindset" in doing your marketing work. It will set you and the brand apart.

BRAND INSIGHT

As a marketer, you don't want to judge what is but what could be. If I told you that I wanted to create a company/brand in the taxi marketplace in 2009 but not buy a fleet of taxi's or hire any drivers, would you have laughed at me? Uber. Let me give you another example. This industry has been around for hundreds of years; however, it started to decline rapidly in the 1980's. The founders of this brand looked at the industry but more importantly, looked at what customers were doing around gaming, entertainment, and travel. Rather than compete with a traditional "brand" in a declining industry, they re-shaped the product and then created a powerful brand that redefined the industry. Cirque du Soleil was born. First as a small show with no marketing which meant they needed word of mouth from consumers to grow. But the "brand" they created was so powerful that customers not only embraced the "product" but redefined their own idea of what a modern circus was supposed to be. In an industry that was dying, Cirque du Soleil created a multi-billion brand with no real competition.

KEY TAKEAWAY

When you want to create a powerful brand in any industry, even a declining one, listen and watch what customers are doing. Use Blue Ocean Strategy to get you going. Then build a brand that re-defines the industry to better meet or exceed customer expectations. People don't get into an Uber with a stranger driving based on a breakthrough innovation. They just hate traditional taxi's.

CHAPTER THIRTEEN
A BRAND PLANNER AND FINAL THOUGHTS.
* * *

The role of branding and marketing has not changed in the past twenty years. What has changed is the marketing mediums and the tools available to marketers. I wish I was active in creating or marketing a brand today. In my career, the idea of creating a brand out of "thin air" would have seemed impossible but now I am seeing hundreds of brands being created that have no physical company or retail space nor will you meet a company employee. Brands like Uber, AirBnb, Amazon, Shopify, DropBox and so on. These are amazing times for marketers who are able to move faster, be more disruptive and opportunistic and seemingly create brands out of thin air. But you can't be a solid marketer in this new world without really understanding branding. Being a marketer today with no core strategic brand foundation is like giving a child a firehose and asking him to water the house plants. It's a funny thought but this is what marketers today, without strategic intent or brand knowledge, are actually doing in marketplaces all over the world. In order to better understand branding, you need to create a plan.

YOU NEED A PLAN TO BUILD A BRAND
It can be hard to know where to start when faced with a product, brand or client that needs some strategic brand thinking. In order to help you,

I created BrandPlanr, a simple branding tool to help you organize your information with regards to branding a product, service or company. After years of working with brands, I narrowed it down to nine key elements that you need to identify and get answers to in order to begin to create or support the brand. You really can't do any marketing until you complete some kind of brand analysis and hopefully the BrandPlanr will help you. Working with brands can get very complicated. Managers and clients can be difficult to pin down and this tool will help spark the right conversations. I purposely kept this tool simple to help you get started. Here are the nine key elements:

- Brand value: this has to be something uniquely yours that you can defend (i.e. twice the power, waterproof, etc.)
- Brand promise: this is the actual product or service "promise" you are making to current or potential customers (i.e. get your job done faster, etc.)
- Brand persona: use this to describe your brand as a person (i.e. an athlete who moves quickly, driven but with integrity and passion, etc.)
- Brand position: this is your positioning goal either on a category ladder or in the marketplace (i.e. for people who want to be healthy, Vitamin Water gives you vitamins, etc.)
- Brand identity: this is your logo, type face, colors, imagery and graphics
- Brand research: complete a brand analysis competitive quadrant to understand where you are placing this product or service in the marketplace
- Target segment: these are your target customers, primary and secondary
- Customer feeling: this is what people will say about your brand when you are not in the room
- Brand marketing: this is the marketing campaign you will put together to launch and build the brand

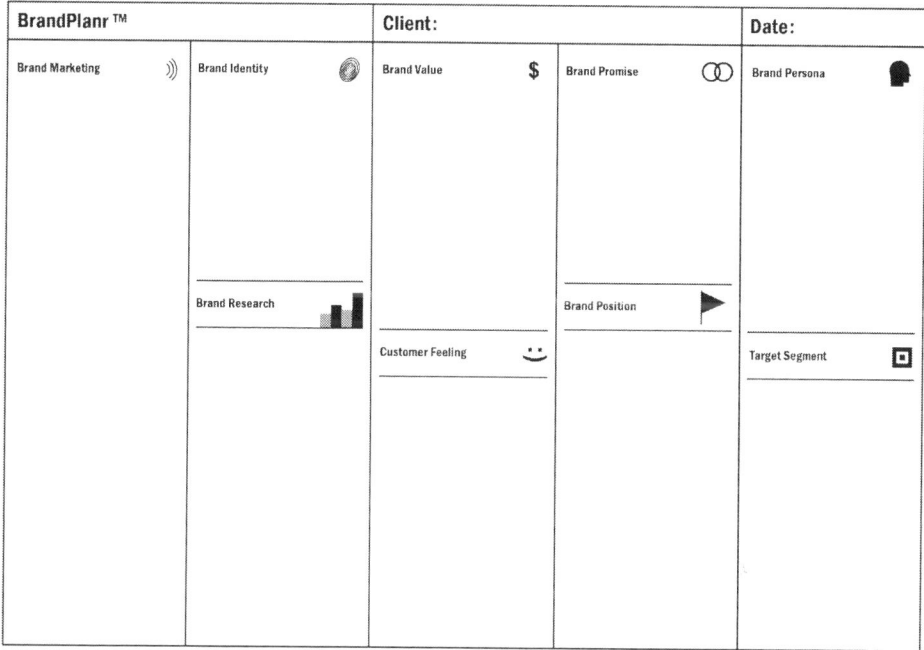

BrandPlanr ™	Client:	Date:
Brand Marketing)))	Brand Value $	Brand Persona 👤
Brand Identity 🔘	Brand Promise ⊙⊙	
		Brand Position ⚑
Brand Research 📊	Customer Feeling ☺	Target Segment ▣

BrandPlanr™ & Copyright 2017

Like I mentioned before, technology is having a massive impact on today's era. This is why I created BrandPlanr as a web app for your laptop, tablet or phone giving you maximum flexibility and access.

I know what you are thinking. This seems like such a simple brand planner. In my twenty years of marketing I have never seen anyone use something like this. We either created a $500,000 brand research audit or we creatively "argued" with managers or the client to eventually get to a place where everyone roughly agreed on the brand strategy. Sophisticated brands and corporate identity firms have a strong branding process with several steps to be completed over four-six months. The rest of us now have the BrandPlanr. At the very minimum, it can get people to quickly agree on what has to be answered in order to move forward with a branding strategy. While I have copyrighted and trademarked BrandPlanr, you can access this branding tool at www.bernieschroeder.com.

CURIOSITY, KNOWLEDGE AND EXPERIENCE

Here is my final advice and parting thoughts in this book that will hopefully have you continue your journey toward becoming a brand expert. I am giving you this advice not because I think I am smarter than you; I just have more curiosity, knowledge and experience. Also, honestly, I want you to be the best possible marketer you can be. Here are my final bits of advice:

- Be curious. If you are going to be a good marketer, you have to know what's going on around you, in the marketplace and across industries. Be more curious on purpose. Walk into stores you have never gone in before, take a different route to work, attend a trade show event based on a new trend, read more books and acquire more understanding and knowledge of trends.

- Have a mentor. My three mentors made my marketing career. I have no clue where I would have ended up without them. Funny thing is, none of them became my long term friends. Good mentors are not necessarily your friends. They are people who care about your professional success, who will have honest and sometimes harsh conversations with you. At other times, they are your best cheerleader. Most importantly, they will allow you to become more strategic as mentors always look at the big picture.

- Work for a wizard. If you are in marketing and are not working for an amazing marketer, make a change. The only way you can learn and grow is to work with someone who will give you the benefit of their knowledge, experience and advice in order to hone your skills. If you are working for someone and you have more knowledge and are smarter than them with respect to marketing, you are learning nothing that will make you better.

- Understand the why. Understand why you work for the brand or company you do, why you work for your manager and why you actually get up every day. In my career, I did not define what I did everyday as "work." I loved marketing so much that I just wanted to be better. I wanted to be a brand expert who could walk into a room, understand the situation and lead a team to build something magnificent.

- Understand branding. If everyone could be a brand expert easily, everyone would become one. The reality is that it's hard to rise in marketing to where you become a brand expert. It takes 5-10 years of hard progressive marketing work, a great mentor, a strong amount of curiosity and the ability to constantly challenge yourself to the point of failure.

- Be more strategic. Executing on marketing tactics is easy. Create this video, post that tweet, slam that ad into Facebook, etc. But what's the real goal? Are you trying to drive customer engagement, brand or product awareness, sales, what? Understand the bigger picture. What's happening in the marketplace, what brand position are you striving for, what trend is fueling your brand's potential growth, where is the blue ocean?

- Build your network. After I interviewed and landed my first marketing job after college, I never submitted my resume for another opportunity again in my entire career. My first mentor counseled me on the power of a network and I built my network relentlessly. After about five years, my name started to appear in news articles, I started speaking at events and the marketing campaigns I was creating were winning awards and growing brands. All my future opportunities came to me through my network as referrals from people that knew me and knew what I was looking for in my career.

- Pay attention to trends. Clients can pay you $100,000 to execute a marketing campaign. Or they can pay you $10,000,000 to craft a brand strategy. Most times clients will ask you to take their brand to a place in the marketplace where they can thrive. How will you know where that is? Paying close attention to top trends might allow you to intersect certain trends or connect some dots to determine where markets or customers are going. If you get good at that, you will be very valuable.

- Develop your gut instinct. A gut instinct is critical to a marketer. There will be times when you evaluate all the information you have and it will not point clearly one way or the other. Then you need to decide. How will you do that? A gut instinct is not a guess. It's a "feeling" that based on knowledge, experience, skills, similar but different situations that will help you decide what to do when someone needs to decide. Practice on smaller decisions in your career before you attempt to make bets on big decisions.

- Enjoy the journey. Early in my career, I worked crazy hours and I loved it. But I also got tired and started to realize I needed to do a good job on "today" as tomorrow would always be there. With that attitude, I went from worrying about how to sell another Mercedes to sleeping like a baby. This mental shift lowered my stress and allowed me to understand that I needed to have "fun" in my career. I learned that I could work hard and play hard and enjoy life. The same goes for you. You need to enjoy the ride.

Here are some books you should read for a variety of reasons. They are in no special order. But they all have some knowledge you need to acquire in your journey of becoming a marketing or brand expert.

Positioning: The Battle for Your Mind, by Al Reis and Jack Trout

Tipping Point, by Malcolm Gladwell

Ogilvy on Advertising, by David Ogilvy

Spin Selling, by Neil Rackham

Brand Gap, by Marty Neumeier

Crossing the Chasm, by Geoffrey A. Moore

How to Win Friends & Influence People, by Dale Carnegie

Where the Suckers Moon, by Randall Rothenberg

As a marketer, you owe it to yourself to never stop learning. And if you are going to become a brand expert, then put in the time and learn your craft. Trust your instinct and trust yourself to be great. Remember to enjoy the ride.

"Keep away from people who try to belittle your ambitions. Small people always do that, but the really great make you feel that you, too, can become great."
- ***MARK TWAIN***

INDEX

✳ ✳ ✳

A

Activation energy, 54
Advertising, 23, 35, 60, 105
Advice, 165
Amazon, 15, 22, 28, 38, 47, 112, 122
Apple, 34, 59, 74, 95, 107
Asset, 45, 58-59
Authenticity, 73, 75-76

B

Baby boomers, 48, 133-134
Bar chart, 86
Barnes & Noble, 22
Blue Ocean Strategy, 68, 128, 136-138
Border, 16, 22, 52, 131
Brand
    Attributes, 15, 66, 80
    Building a, 84-85, 157
    Elements of a, 33-35, 66-67
    Experts, 28, 90, 165-167
    Insights, 7, 19, 55
    Loyalty, 18, 24, 27
    Persona, 15, 34, 163
    Promise, 15, 31-32, 66, 163
Brand rainbow, 80-81
    Strategy, 16, 38, 64, 75,92, 110
Brand advocate, 21, 74
Brand architecture, 90
Brand porfolio strategy, 92, 146, 150
Brand rationale hierarchy, 20-21
BrandPlanr, 163

C

Category ladder, 106-108, 117
Choice, 25-26, 118,
CKS Partners, 16, 103, 152, 170, 180
Clutter, 59, 105, 115
Community, 75
Concierge mentality, 39
Consumer ladder, 123, 129
Content, 42-43
CRM (customer relationship
    management), 71
Crowdsourcing, 75, 85
CSR (corporate social responsibility), 57
Culture, 25, 74, 80
Customer
    Behavior, 16, 44, 156
    Centric-meaning, 158
    Experience, 43-46, 82
    Experts, 9
    Feeling, 8, 16-19, 26, 31, 103, 163
    Insights, 9, 14, 38, 44, 68
    Mind, 109-110, 124-125
    Rationale, 20-21
    Truth, 10, 38-39
    Value, 17, 26, 113, 150

D

Data centralization, 44
Decision trees, 89, 95-97
Demographics, 72, 111
Differentiators, 56, 89-90
Digital marketer, 9, 14, 23-24, 44,
    78, 89-90

Digital marketing mistakes, 41-45
Digital world, 15
Disruption, 39, 129, 141
Distribution channels, 27, 144, 146

E

Ecommerce, 47, 146-147
Emotional benefit, 59-60
Emotional connection, 17-19, 103
Emotional feeling, 15, 60
Emotional value, 19
Ethnography, 10

F

Focus groups, 10, 71,
Four P'S of marketing, 144-146, 148

G

Google, 35, 126
GoPro, 52-53,
Graphing, 72
Gut instinct, 25, 98, 167

H

Harvard Business Review, 21, 120
History of
    Branding, 26-28
    Four P's, 145
Hot buttons, 71
House of brands, 90, 94-95

I

IMC (intograted marketing
    communications), 154, 157-159
    Benefits, 159-160
Influencer, 15
Insights, 19, 109, 134-135
    Key insights, 49

Trend insights, 16, 132
Integrated marketing, 103, 152-155, 157
Internet, 28, 129-130, 146
IPO (initial public offering), 154

K

KPI (critical performance indicators), 42

L

Lifetime value, 17
Logo, 25, 33-34, 37, 97

M

Marketing
    Brand marketing, 53-54, 163
    Product marketing, 25, 52-54
    Digital marketing, 8, 40-43, 106, 159,
    Strategy, 8, 17, 44, 64, 70
    Agency, 16, 64, 103, 129, 154
Marketplace, 39-40, 46, 117
Mascot, 55-56, 57
Mass media, 27, 157
Mass production, 27
Master brand, 92, 97
Mentorship, 30, 165-166
Millennials, 48, 133-136, 147
Misconceptions, 23-24
Mission statement (*see also*
    positioning statement), 31
Mixers, 145
Multi-channel strategy, 43

N

Network, 131-132, 166
Niche, 39, 55, 141
Non-leading questions, 14

INDEX CONTINUED...

✳ ✳ ✳

O

Observation lab, 9-12, 15, 68
Observational research, 10
Observing, 10, 12-13, 68
Ownership, 26-27, 91

P

Path analysis, 15
Pay at the pump, 13
Perception map, 69-71
Positioning, 34, 102-106
Positioning statement (*see also* mission statement), 108-113
Process steps, 110
Price, 54, 92
Product categories, 19, 117, 119

R

Red Ocean strategy, 138, 140
Report card, 86-87
Retention strategy, 18,
ROBI (return on brand investment), 160
ROI (return on investment), 44, 75, 160

S

SEO, 159
Silos, 41, 43
Social media, 28, 53, 135
Sponsorship, 153, 158
Storytelling, 56, 82-83
Subscription business model, 19, 73, 127

T

Tagline, 31, 109, 113,
Tangible, 34, 58, 67
Target audience, 24, 73, 81, 87, 93, 105
Target customer, 111
Trademark, 27, 164,
Trends, 119, 128-130, 165-166
Trendspotting, 131-132
Tips for, 131-133
Trust, 26, 58, 168

U

USP (unique selling proposition), 59

V

VC (venture capitalist), 64, 170
Visual identity, 25, 33

W

Whole activity, 14

X

X-factor, 25

ABOUT THE AUTHOR

* * *

Bernhard Schroeder brings over 20 years of branding, marketing and entrepreneurial experience, both as a senior partner in a global integrated marketing agency and as a former chief marketing officer on the client side. Today, Bernhard is a Director at the Lavin Entrepreneurship Center at San Diego State University, where he oversees all of the Center's undergraduate and graduate experiential programs. In 2017, San Diego State University was named the National Model Undergraduate Entrepreneurship Program for 2017 by the United States Association for Small Business and Entrepreneurship. Past rankings include 18th on FORBES most entrepreneurial universities list. He has worked with hundreds of start-ups in the San Diego area, on and off the campus.

He is a strategic adviser/mentor to several start-ups and is quoted frequently in both local and national media and has spoken at TEDx events. He also teaches several entrepreneurship courses (Creativity and Innovation, Entrepreneurship Fundamentals, Business Model/Plan Development for Entrepreneurs) within the Fowler College of Business at San Diego State University.

Since moving to San Diego in 1997, he has specialized in working with entrepreneurs and venture capitalists in either growth or turnaround opportunities, with several companies ranging from $40 million to $250 million. Prior to moving to San Diego, Bernhard was a senior partner in the world's largest integrated marketing communications agency, CKS Partners, which in 1998 had offices in over 30 countries, more than 10,000 employees, and over $1 billion in revenue. He had joined CKS in 1991, when the firm had only 16 employees and just $1.7 million in revenue. He opened the first out-of-state agency office for CKS in 1993 in Portland, Oregon, and working with the other partners, grew the firm to almost $40 million in revenue by 1995, and led CKS to a successful initial public offering that same year. Bernhard has marketing, operational, and entrepreneurship experience working with Fortune 100 firms like Apple, Nike, General Motors, American Express, Mercedes Benz, and Kellogg's, as well as start-up companies. He was involved in the initial branding and marketing launches for online companies like Yahoo!, Amazon.com, Corbis, and ESPN SportsZone. The agency worked with many key brands like Levi's, Audi, Williams Sonoma, McDonalds, United Airlines, eBay, Pixar, Timberland, Harley Davidson, Microsoft, and Visa.

OTHER BOOKS BY THIS AUTHOR

In addition to Brands and Bulls**t, Bernhard Schroeder has written two other thought provoking books on entrepreneurship and creativity.

This book is written for the person who feels they should be an entrepreneur but don't know how to get started. Schroeder demystifies entrepreneruship and breaks it down into several easy to get started steps. Full of insights and learnings to help you get started now!

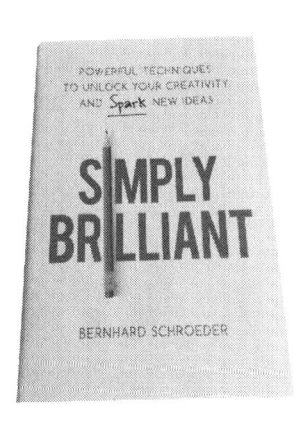

The world rewards and provides opportunities to people who can creatively solve problems. The good news? *We are all creative.* Learn how to get your creativity back and flowing on purpose with this powerful book and build the career you deserve.

Printed in Poland
by Amazon Fulfillment
Poland Sp. z o.o., Wrocław